A Child's Introduction to
NORSE MYTHOLOGY

A Child's Introduction to
NORSE MYTHOLOGY

Odin, Thor, Loki, and Other Viking
Gods, Goddesses, Giants, and Monsters

By Heather Alexander

Illustrated by Meredith Hamilton

BLACK DOG
& LEVENTHAL
PUBLISHERS
NEW YORK

Black Dog & Leventhal Publishers
Hachette Book Group
1290 Avenue of the Americas
New York, NY 10104
www.hachettebookgroup.com
www.blackdogandleventhal.com

First Edition: October 2018
Black Dog & Leventhal Publishers is an imprint of Running Press, a division of Hachette Book Group.
The Black Dog & Leventhal Publishers name and logo are trademarks of Hachette Book Group, Inc.

The publisher is not responsible for websites (or their content) that are not owned by the publisher.
The Hachette Speakers Bureau provides a wide range of authors for speaking events.
To find out more, go to www.HachetteSpeakersBureau.com or call (866) 376-6591.

Print book interior design by Sheila Hart Design
Fact checking by Gantt Gurley

Library of Congress Control Number: 2018931237
ISBNs: 978-0-316-48215-8 (hardcover), 978-0-316-41793-8 (ebook), 978-0-316-41806-5 (KF8), 978-0-316-41805-8 (EPIB)

Printed in China
APS
10 9 8 7 6 5 4

For Lisa Tenaglia, editor extraordinaire!

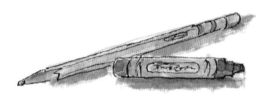

A NOTE TO PARENTS AND EDUCATORS

The Norse myths tackle life's big issues: love, death, loyalty, courage, vengeance, and justice. Many epic battles contribute to the myths' excitement. The battles are certainly violent (fought with spears and magical weapons), but the violence is more often than not directed toward giants and other mythological creatures. The Norse gods do not live monogamous lives (the enclosed family tree will help you sort it all out), but the gods' and goddesses' many children are well cared for and loved. The Norse myths are some of the most engaging and memorable stories to read together. While the myths can be read out of order, they make better sense if you read them beginning to end. We hope you enjoy them.

CONTENTS

PART 2: THE MYTHS

Norse Mythology and the Vikings

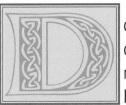o you like magical worlds, super-strong warriors, wise gods, clever goddesses, gruesome giants, sneaky dwarves, and menacing dragons? If you said yes, you'll love Norse mythology. In this book, we visit lands of ice and fire, witness epic battles, delight in devious trickery, hear tales of love and honor, and learn how the world began . . . and how it will end.

What Is a Myth?

Myths are stories. The myths in this book were first told more than 1,200 years ago. Myths helped ancient people make sense of their confusing world.

Imagine you lived in a time long before the Internet, telephones, or even libraries. You see a jagged bolt of fire flash through the sky during a storm. You're scared, because no one can explain what it is. The science is not understood yet. Lightning, thunder, and rain are all mysterious. Then someone tells a story about the super-strong, red-haired god Thor, who hurls his hammer across the sky to kill evil giants. Suddenly, the flash of fire makes sense. His hammer caused that bolt of light. The story gives you courage. That's what many myths aim to do.

Many of your favorite movies, TV shows, and comic books borrow from famous Norse myths. Why? Norse myths are filled with edge-of-your seat action and fascinating characters. Norse gods act like the people you know: Odin is like your wise teacher; Loki is like your mischievous friend, dragging you into trouble; and Thor is like your hot-tempered uncle who always has your back. But most of all, a really good story is a really good story—no matter if it was told thousands of years ago or today. And the Norse myths are really good stories!

WHAT IS NORSE?

Norse is an ancient language spoken by Norsemen, or "people from the North." Norsemen were also known as **Vikings**. The Vikings came from three modern-day countries in northern Europe: Denmark, Norway, and Sweden. Grouped together, these countries are called **Scandinavia**.

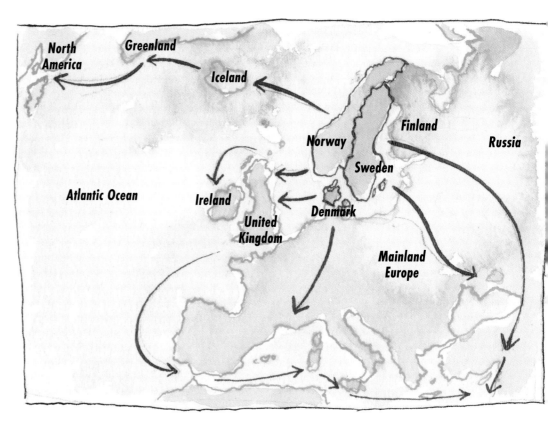

WHO WERE THE VIKINGS?

The Vikings were farmers, traders, and fishermen. Very little of Scandinavia's soil was good for farming and there wasn't enough food to feed all the people, so the Vikings traveled to Iceland, Greenland, Britain, France, Russia—and even America. They landed in North America about 500 years before Christopher Columbus. They traveled farther than any European people before them.

The Vikings were fierce fighters. They raided monasteries and burned down villages, stealing treasures and taking over land. People feared the Vikings.

The Age of the Vikings lasted from roughly 793 to 1066 CE. The Vikings ruled the seas and conquered much land. Then the Christians defeated the Vikings and took over.

ABOUT THE MYTHS

The Vikings prized bravery and physical strength, but they also celebrated storytellers. Scandinavian winters were bitterly cold and lonely, and the skies stayed dark for months. It was the perfect weather to sit around a cozy fire in a big hall and tell tales. Norse myths were passed on by word of mouth. Many myths were told in the form of poems, which helped storytellers remember them.

IF YOUR FAMILY COMES FROM NORTHERN EUROPE, YOU MOST LIKELY HAVE SOME VIKING BLOOD IN YOU!

Many Norse myths were forgotten, because they had not been written down. They were replaced with stories from the Christian Bible. However, in Iceland, unknown poets in the 1200s wrote a book of poems about the myths, called the *Poetic Edda*. Then an Icelandic chieftain named Snorri Sturluson explained these poems in the *Prose Edda*, which became the basis for the Norse myths we know today.

Vikings were skilled at building long, thin boats called longships. Longships moved quickly when rowed by oars but also had square sails. They could be sailed in shallow water, land on beaches, and travel up rivers. This made them great for battle.

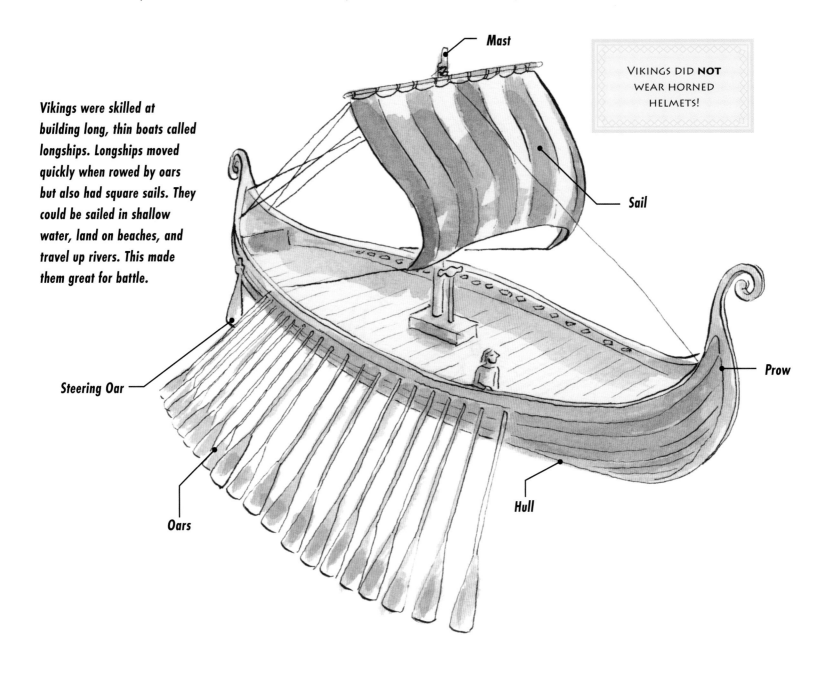

Mast

VIKINGS DID **NOT** WEAR HORNED HELMETS!

Sail

Prow

Steering Oar

Hull

Oars

IN THE BEGINNING . . .

Every group of people has a story to explain how the world was created. This is how it all began for the Vikings.

Before there was anything—any people, any animals, any sky, any seas, any noise—there were only fire and ice.

To the south was **Muspell**, the realm of fire. Searing flames burned and sparked, giving off the most intense heat. Nothing could live here.

To the north was **Niflheim**, the realm of ice. Icicles and frost covered the land, holding the gray mist in a deep freeze. Nothing could live here.

In between lay a great empty space called **Ginnungagap**.

Eleven poisonous rivers of ice snaked through Niflheim and reached across Ginnungagap. As they neared the heat of Muspell, the ice began to melt. Water dripped, and the drips formed **Ymir**, the first frost giant, and **Audumla**, a huge cow without horns. The giant and the cow were both bigger than you'd ever dare to imagine.

Ymir slept, and as he slept, he sweated. His children were born from his sweat. A male and female giant came from under his left arm. A six-headed giant came from his legs. From these three nasty, ugly giants, other giants were born.

Meanwhile, Audumla licked a salty block of ice. On the first day, a man's hair emerged from the ice. On the second day, his head came out. On the third day, his full body appeared. His name was **Buri**. Unlike Ymir's children, he was tall, handsome, and good. Buri and one of the frost giants had a son called **Bor**. Bor married **Bestla**, also a giant, and they had three sons: **Odin**, **Vili**, and **Ve**. They were the first gods.

The three brothers grew up in the emptiness of Ginnungagap. They wanted to build a world of living things. Ymir refused. He and his children were wicked and violent, and the brothers hated them. Odin knew Ymir must die in order for the world to begin. Odin stabbed the evil frost giant. Ymir's blood drowned all the evil frost giants except Ymir's grandson **Bergelmir** and his wife. They sailed away in a hollowed-out tree trunk. They are thought to be the father and mother of all giants. The giants never forgave the gods for the death of Ymir and became their deadly enemies.

Odin, Vili, and Ve threw Ymir's body into Ginnungagap, and from his remains, they made the world. His flesh was turned into soil. His bones became the mountains. His teeth became rocks. His hair became trees. His blood became the sea. They tossed his skull up high to make the sky. His brains floated out to become the clouds. The three brothers shot sparks from Muspell into the sky to be the stars. They placed a goddess named Sun and a god named Moon into two chariots of fire. Sun and Moon are chased across the sky by two savage wolves who try to eat them. Night, the daughter of a giant, and her son, Day, were given horse-drawn chariots to ride in, too. Every twenty-four hours, they have to make a circle around the world.

The brothers divided up the land. They gave the giants the rocky coastlines to the north and called it **Jotunheim**. They dug up worms in soil that had been Ymir's flesh and turned them into dwarves and Dark Elves. They sent them to live deep underground in **Nidavellir** and **Svartalfheim**. They made a land called **Alfheim** for the Light Elves. The middle of the earth was called **Midgard**. The gods built a wall around it from Ymir's eyebrows to keep out the giants. Midgard had green meadows, rushing rivers, sandy beaches, majestic mountains, and a blue sky. But it was empty. A land this beautiful needed life.

One day, the brothers were walking along the beach and came upon logs from two trees—an ash and an elm. With a *whoosh*, Odin breathed life into them. Ve carved them into the shape of people. He let them see, hear, and speak. Vili gave them thoughts and feelings. The ash tree became **Ask**, the first man. The elm tree became **Embla**, the first woman. Ask and Embla are the father and mother of all humans.

Odin and his brothers left the humans to live in Midgard. They crossed the **Bifrost**, a glittery rainbow bridge, to a world high above the earth called **Asgard**. The brothers found wives, had children, and soon filled Asgard with gods and goddesses.

Finally, everything and everyone was in its place.

But in a world of gods, giants, dwarves, and elves, all was not peaceful. There were battles to fight, injustices to avenge, wrongs to right, and tricks to play.

The World Tree

**ggdrasil** is the mighty tree that stands in the center of the universe. The tree grows forever green, and its sturdy branches touch the very top of the sky. Its twisting roots and branches support the nine worlds that make up the universe, so it is called the World Tree. Everything is connected through Yggdrasil.

Yggdrasil has three enormous roots. One reaches into Asgard, land of the gods, one reaches into Jotunheim, land of the giants, and one reaches into Niflheim, land of the dead. A spring flows under each root. The poisonous **Spring of Hvergelmir** pools under Niflheim. The spring of wisdom, called **Mimir's Well**, sits under Jotunheim. The **Well of Urd**, the spring of fate, bubbles under Asgard.

The Well of Urd is cared for by three giantess sisters called the **Norns**. It's their job to feed Yggdrasil with water from the Well of Urd to keep the universe healthy. The Norns also decide what will happen to you throughout your life. They weave a tapestry, and each thread in the tapestry is the fate of a single human or god.

ANIMALS IN THE WORLD TREE

Many animals live in the World Tree. A wise eagle called **Hraesvelg** sits on the top, keeping close watch on the universe from his high perch. A hawk stands between his eyes. When Hraesvelg beats his wings, he makes the wind blow. The evil serpent-dragon **Nidhogg** gnaws at the tree's roots, trying to destroy the tree so the world will fall apart. **Ratatosk** the squirrel scurries up and down the trunk, delivering insults between the eagle and the serpent, who hate each other. (Warning: Do not trust the squirrel. He tells lies.) Four deer that represent the four winds gallop on the tree's branches and eat the buds.

The Nine Worlds

sgard is the land of the **Aesir**, the gods and goddesses of war. Asgard sits high in the clouds, and each god lives in a gorgeous gold-and-silver hall. The shimmering roofs of the halls cast a magical glow throughout the land.

VALHALLA IS A PART OF ODIN'S MAGNIFICENT HALL IN ASGARD. ITS GOLDEN ROOF IS MADE FROM WARRIORS' SHIELDS AND IS HELD UP BY SPEARS. NOBLE WARRIORS WHO DIE HEROICALLY IN BATTLE ARE BROUGHT TO VALHALLA BY THE **VALKYRIES**. THE VALKYRIES ARE BEAUTIFUL WOMEN WHO RIDE WINGED HORSES. THEY DECIDE WHO LIVES AND DIES DURING BATTLE. THEY BRING HALF THE DEAD WARRIORS TO VALHALLA. THE DEAD ENTER VALHALLA THROUGH ENORMOUS DOORS THAT CAN FIT ONE THOUSAND WARRIORS. EVERY NIGHT, THE HEROES ENJOY AN ENORMOUS FEAST OF MEAT AND MEAD. ODIN SITS AT THE HEAD OF THE HALL.

Vanaheim is the land of the **Vanir**, the fertility gods and goddesses. Vanaheim is a mysterious world that some say is filled with gray, swirling mist.

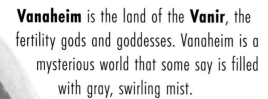

Alfheim is the land of the Light Elves, who are happy and kind.

THE BIFROST IS THE RAINBOW BRIDGE THAT CONNECTS ASGARD TO MIDGARD. IT IS THE ONLY ENTRANCE. IF YOU SEE A RAINBOW, IT MEANS A NORSE GOD HAS COME TO VISIT! **HEIMDALL** IS THE WATCHMAN OF THE BRIDGE.

Midgard, also known as Earth, is the land of the humans. It is surrounded by oceans so wide and so deep that no human can cross to the other side. **Jormungand**, the horrible serpent, lives in the ocean. Midgard is the only visible world, meaning the only world that humans can see.

Nidavellir is the land of the dwarves. Dwarves live underground in caves and holes connected by a labyrinth of tunnels. They are highly skilled craftsmen and blacksmiths who can make any weapon or treasure.

Svartalfheim is the land of the Dark Elves.

Jotunheim is the land of the frost giants. It's covered with rugged mountains, icy peaks, thick forests, and swirling snowstorms.

The giants' fortress, **Utgard**, is made from huge blocks of ice. The **Iron Woods** separate the giants from the humans in Midgard. The **River Ifing**, which never freezes over, separates the giants from the gods in Asgard.

WHY DO THE NAMES OF MOST OF THE NINE WORLDS END WITH EITHER "-HEIM" OR "-GARD"?

HEIM MEANS "HOUSE," "HOME," OR "WORLD." THE TWO WORLDS ENDING WITH *-GARD* (ASGARD AND MIDGARD) HAVE WALLS AROUND THEM. THE VIKINGS BELIEVED THIS MADE THEM MORE ORDERLY.

Niflheim is the land of the dead. It sits below all the other worlds. The sky is blanketed by a thick fog, and it's always bitter cold, damp, and dark. No joy or happiness can exist here. Humans who die of accidents, sickness, or old age end up here. **Hel** is the queen of Niflheim.

Muspell is the land of fire. It is filled with blazing flames and scorching-hot embers and coals. The evil demon **Surt** rules Muspell. He carries a flaming sword that burns hotter than the sun.

Gods and Goddesses

Norse gods are different from the gods you may have read about in Greek and Roman mythology. They're much more like humans. They experience pain, sadness, fear, jealousy, and joy. They get hungry. They play tricks. They make bad choices. Unlike Greek and Roman gods, Norse gods and goddesses don't live forever. Endings are not always happy for them. With the Norse gods and goddesses, anything can happen.

Knowing the End at the Beginning

It's kind of like reading the last line of a story first. Throughout the Norse myths, we know that the end will come. There will be a final battle between the gods and goddesses and giants and monsters. This battle is called **Ragnarok**. It is a battle between good and evil, and it will destroy the world. Odin sees the future and knows Ragnarok is coming, but there's nothing he, or any god, can do to stop it. Gods and humans will die, the Sun will go dark, stars will fall from the sky, and the seas will swallow the land. But the Sun will give birth to a daughter, and the world will start again.

The Vikings believed Ragnarok to be a good thing. It allowed the gods to stop evil from invading the world. They believed that life and death made a big circle, and after death, everything was reborn.

Aesir and Vanir

The Norse gods and goddesses are divided into two groups—the Aesir and the Vanir. At first, the two groups fought brutal battles against each other. Then they declared peace and came together against the giants.

DAYS OF THE WEEK

DID YOU KNOW THAT MOST DAYS OF THE WEEK ARE NAMED AFTER NORSE GODS AND GODDESSES?

SUNDAY = SUN'S DAY
MONDAY = MOON'S DAY
TUESDAY = TYR'S DAY
WEDNESDAY = WODEN'S DAY
("WODEN" IS ODIN IN OLD ENGLISH.)
THURSDAY = THOR'S DAY
FRIDAY = FREYA'S DAY
(SATURDAY WAS NAMED AFTER THE ROMAN GOD SATURN.)

Odin

Odin is the most powerful Norse god and the supreme ruler. He's the god of wisdom, poetry, and battle. He's the creator of humans.

OTHER NAMES: The All-Father (he's the father of all the gods), God of the Skies, Raven God, Lord of Asgard

FAMILY: Odin is married to **Frigg**. His sons are **Thor**, **Balder**, **Hod**, **Hermod**, **Váli**, and **Vidar**. **Bragi**, **Tyr**, and **Heimdall** may also be his sons. **Loki** is his "oath-brother." They weren't born as brothers, but they made a pact always to be brothers.

HOME: A sparkly palace in Asgard called **Gladsheim**. He sits on his golden throne and watches over the nine worlds.

DID YOU KNOW?

Odin wanders Midgard, land of the humans, disguised as an old man. He wears a wide-brimmed hat and carries a staff. Humans who are kind to him receive wealth and happiness. Humans who are mean or ignore him end up with bad fortune and misery.

ANIMALS: Odin has two ravens—**Hugin** ("Thought") and **Munin** ("Memory")—that fly around the world every day. At night, they perch on Odin's shoulder and whisper into his ear what every god, giant, human, and living thing is up to—good or bad. Odin rides **Sleipnir**, an eight-legged gray horse who is the fastest horse in the world. Two wolves—**Geri** ("Greedy") and **Freki** ("Ravenous")—sit by his feet, and because Odin doesn't need to eat, he feeds them his food.

MAGICAL OBJECTS: Odin's magical spear, **Gungnir**, never misses its target. Odin can start a battle on earth by throwing it. **Draupnir**, his arm ring, makes eight other gold rings every nine nights.

POWERS:

WISDOM: Odin gave up one of his eyes to drink from the Well of Knowledge. He hung from the branches of Yggdrasil for nine days to understand mysterious writings called the runes. Odin believes the quest for knowledge is worth pain and sacrifice.

POETRY: Odin stole a drink called the Mead of Poetry from the giants, and it gave him the power of poetry. When he offers a human a sip, he or she will become a talented poet.

COURAGE: In battle, Odin gives warriors the bravery to fight.

LOOKS & ATTITUDE: Odin has one eye, white hair, and a long beard. He's sometimes stern, and very wise. He values courage.

THOR

Thor is the god of thunder and the protector of mankind. He is the bravest and strongest of all the gods.

OTHER NAMES: The Thunderer, Defender of Asgard

FAMILY: Thor's father is Odin, and his mother is **Jord**, goddess of the earth. He's Odin's oldest son. His wife is the golden-haired **Sif**, goddess of the harvest. Their daughter, **Thrud**, is a Valkyrie. With a giantess, Thor had two sons, **Magni** and **Modi**.

HOME: His hall in Asgard is **Bilskirnir**. It is the largest building ever built.

ANIMALS: He rides a bronze chariot driven by two goats, **Toothgnasher** and **Toothgrinder**. The goats grind their teeth so fiercely that sparks fly. When they race across the sky, their chariot causes thunder to rumble.

MAGICAL OBJECTS: Mjollnir is Thor's mighty hammer. When he slams down Mjollnir, lightning flashes. It can crush the skull of the most enormous giant. Thor's hammer always comes back to him after striking an enemy.

Thor wears magical iron gloves that allow him to hold his heavy hammer and catch it when it returns.

He also wears a magical belt called **Megingjord** that doubles his strength.

LOOKS & ATTITUDE: Thor has red flowing hair and a red beard. He's big and muscular. He will fight any giant or any monster. He has a fiery temper but doesn't stay angry for long. Straightforward and loyal, Thor expects others to act the same. He loves to eat and drink.

MANY VIKINGS WORE SMALL COPIES OF THOR'S MAGIC HAMMER AROUND THEIR NECKS FOR PROTECTION.

DID YOU KNOW?
Thor's arch-enemy is **Jormungand,** the Midgard serpent.

Loki

oki is known for playing tricks and practical jokes.

OTHER NAMES: The Trickster, God of Mischief

FAMILY: Loki is not an Aesir or a Vanir. Both his parents were giants. He was raised as Odin's oath-brother. His wife is **Sigyn**. With the giantess **Angrboda**, he has three horrible children: **Fenrir** (a scary wolf), Jormungand (the hissing Midgard serpent), and **Hel** (the goddess of death). He is also the mother (yes, the mother!) of Sleipnir, Odin's eight-legged horse.

HOME: Asgard

ANIMALS: Loki doesn't have any special animals, but he's the father of some terrifying ones!

MAGICAL OBJECTS: Loki has no magical objects, but he can change shape. He has turned into a fish, a fly, a horse, and a woman.

LOOKS & ATTITUDE: Unlike the ugly giants, Loki is handsome and smaller. Loki is mischievous, clever, and full of devious ideas. He both annoys and delights the gods with his tricks and cheating. He helps the gods, but, at the same time, he can be spiteful and wicked. Loki does whatever is best for Loki.

IT'S NORSE, OF COURSE!!

MARVEL HAS A VILLAIN NAMED LOKI WHO FIGHTS THOR AND THE AVENGERS. LOKI ALSO APPEARS IN COMPOSER RICHARD WAGNER'S FAMOUS OPERA *DER RING DES NIBELUNGEN (THE RING OF NIBELUNG)*, COMMONLY KNOWN AS THE RING CYCLE.

Frigg

Frigg is the goddess of the skies and love, and the protector of marriage and children.

OTHER NAMES: Frigga, Goddess of Beauty, Queen of the Gods, Queen of Heaven

FAMILY: Frigg is Odin's favorite wife, and he treats her as a true partner. Balder, Hod, and Hermod are her sons. She tries to save Balder from death but can't.

HOME: She lives in her own palace in Asgard, where many goddesses serve her.

ANIMALS: Her sacred animal is the goose. In Germany, she was the original Mother Goose.

MAGICAL OBJECTS: Frigg spins gold into thread. Many think she weaves the destinies of gods and humans.

LOOKS & ATTITUDE: Beautiful Frigg is very wise. She can see the future, but she will never tell anyone what will happen, nor can she change it. She's an excellent keeper of secrets. She is a loving and caring mother. She watches over all households, helping women with childbirth and their families.

DID YOU KNOW?

Frigg is the only other god allowed to sit on Odin's throne.

WHERE ARE ALL THE GODDESSES?

THERE ARE VERY FEW SURVIVING MYTHS ABOUT THE GODDESSES. HISTORIANS BELIEVE THAT THERE WERE MANY MORE, BUT (MAYBE BECAUSE THEY WERE ABOUT WOMEN) THESE STORIES FAILED TO GET PASSED ON OR WRITTEN DOWN. THE GODDESSES THAT APPEAR IN NORSE MYTHOLOGY ARE STRONG AND SMART. THEY SPEAK THEIR MINDS AND ACT AS EQUALS TO THE MALE GODS.

Balder

Balder is the god of peace and light.

OTHER NAMES: The Beautiful, Fairest of the Gods

FAMILY: His parents are Odin and Frigg. His brothers are Hod and Hermod. He's married to **Nanna**. After Balder dies, Nanna dies of sadness so she can travel with him to the land of the dead. Their son, **Forseti**, is god of justice.

HOME: His hall is in the countryside of Asgard.

LOOKS & ATTITUDE: Balder is handsome with blond hair. He glows with goodness. He likes everyone. All the gods (except Loki) love him.

DID YOU KNOW?
Balder dreamed his own death. This scared his mother so much that she made everything in the world promise not to harm her son. But Loki tricked Hod into killing Balder. The death of Balder was the death of goodness, setting the world on its downward spiral to Ragnarok, the end.

Hod

Hod is the god of darkness and winter.

OTHER NAMES: The Blind God

FAMILY: He is the son of Odin and Frigg. His brothers are Balder and Hermod.

HOME: Asgard

DID YOU KNOW?
Váli, the god of vengeance, killed Hod to avenge Balder's death. Hod and Balder will be reborn after Ragnarok.

LOOKS & ATTITUDE: He's blind, so he never sees the deadly mistletoe that he shoots at Balder. He's gentle and gullible, which made it easier for Loki to trick him. He carries a bow and arrow.

Tyr

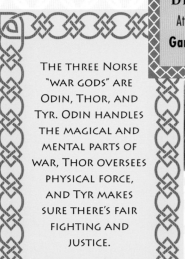

Tyr is the god of justice and the law. He helped create the rules for fighting.

FAMILY: His father is either Odin or the giant **Hymir** (it's different in different myths).

HOME: Asgard

MAGICAL OBJECTS: He's an expert with swords and spears.

LOOKS & ATTITUDE: Tyr is extremely courageous. He's the only god brave enough to put his hand into the wolf Fenrir's mouth. His hand was bitten off, but he sacrificed it to make the world safer. He now has only one hand.

> **DID YOU KNOW?**
> At Ragnarok, Tyr will fight **Garm**, the guard dog of Hel.

> THE THREE NORSE "WAR GODS" ARE ODIN, THOR, AND TYR. ODIN HANDLES THE MAGICAL AND MENTAL PARTS OF WAR, THOR OVERSEES PHYSICAL FORCE, AND TYR MAKES SURE THERE'S FAIR FIGHTING AND JUSTICE.

Heimdall

Heimdall is the watchman of the gods. Heimdall stands at the top of the Bifrost, the rainbow bridge, making sure no giants cross into Asgard.

OTHER NAMES: Guardian of the Gods, God of Protection

> **DID YOU KNOW?**
> Heimdall and Loki are enemies.

FAMILY: He's thought to be the son of nine maidens (who are also the waves in the sea), meaning he has nine mothers! He may also be Odin's son.

HOME: A hall next to the Bifrost

ANIMALS: He rides a golden-maned horse called **Gulltop**.

MAGICAL OBJECTS: He carries a large golden trumpet called **Gjallerhorn**. One blast makes the world shake and the stars quiver. He keeps his horn by Mimir's Well. He will blow it to signal Ragnarok, the end of the world.

LOOKS & ATTITUDE: Heimdall has super senses. He can see in the dark and in hundreds of directions. He can hear each blade of grass grow and the clouds float. He needs almost no sleep—and he's always on watch.

Freya

Freya is the goddess of love and beauty. She is the head of the Valkyries.

FAMILY: Her twin brother is **Frey** and her father is **Njord**.

HOME: Freya lives in her own hall in Asgard. She flies out to the battlefield with the Valkyries. She takes half the heroes killed in battle to her hall and the other half are sent to Odin's Valhalla. Freya gets first pick.

ANIMALS: Freya rides a golden chariot pulled by two large gray cats. Sometimes, she rides a boar.

MAGICAL OBJECTS: She has a magical cape made of falcon feathers. When she puts it on, she can fly.

LOOKS & ATTITUDE: Freya is extremely beautiful, and the giants and dwarves all want to marry her. She is often sad. Her husband, **Od**, mysteriously disappeared, and Freya cries herself to sleep, weeping tears of gold that pool by her feet.

DID YOU KNOW?
Freya wears the **Necklace of the Brisings**, a beautiful, sparkly necklace made by the dwarves. If you look up into the night sky, you can see Freya's necklace. We call it the Milky Way.

IT'S NORSE, OF COURSE!
THE VIKINGS THOUGHT THAT THE AURORA BOREALIS, OR NORTHERN LIGHTS, WAS REALLY THE SHINY ARMOR FREYA AND THE VALKYRIES WEAR WHEN THEY RIDE ACROSS THE SKY TO THE BATTLEFIELDS.

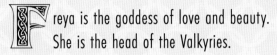

Frey

Frey is the god of the harvest, peace, and good fortune. He controls the sun and rain and makes the crops grow.

FAMILY: His twin sister is Freya and his father is Njord. He marries **Gerd**, daughter of the giantess Angrboda.

HOME: Alfheim, the home of the Light Elves.

ANIMALS: He has a golden boar named **Gullinbursti**, whom the dwarves made for him. His boar pulls his chariot and lights the night sky.

MAGICAL OBJECTS: His magical sword can kill his enemies all by itself. Frey gives his magical sword to his servant so he can marry Gerd. During Ragnarok, he will wish he had his sword when he battles the giant Surt.

LOOKS & ATTITUDE: Frey has long, flowing hair, a stubbly beard, and piercing eyes. He is a noble warrior but prefers peaceful solutions that bring happiness.

DID YOU KNOW?
He rides his magical boat called *Skidbladnir*. This boat always has a favorable wind and can be folded up to fit into a tiny pouch.

Njord

Njord is god of the seas, wind, and navigation. Njord creates favorable winds and guides sailors and fishermen through stormy seas.

FAMILY: Njord is the father of Frey and Freya. His second wife is the giantess and goddess of winter, **Skadi**, who married him because she liked his feet.

HOME: His hall is on the seashore in Asgard. Skadi hates the seagulls by Njord's home, and Njord hates the howling wolves in Skadi's cold mountain home, so they often live apart.

LOOKS & ATTITUDE: He is a gentle mediator.

DID YOU KNOW?
Njord and his children were sent to live in Asgard to keep the peace between the Aesir and the Vanir.

More Gods and Goddesses!

You've met the biggies of Norse mythology, but there are many other gods who appear in minor roles in the stories.

Bragi is the god of poetry. He's married to Idunn. He sings poems to the noble dead in Valhalla.

Idunn is the goddess of youth and keeper of the golden apples of youth. One bite of her apples will keep a god young forever. She's married to Bragi.

Hermod is the messenger god. He may be a son of Odin. He courageously volunteers to travel to the land of the dead to bring back Balder.

Hoenir is a handsome Aesir who's sent to be the chieftain of the Vanir. He has the looks but not the brains for the job.

Mimir is an extremely wise god. His name means "memory." His head gets cut off from his body, yet he still guards Mimir's Well, also called the Well of Knowledge.

Aegir and **Ran** are married sea gods. Their nine daughters make the waves of the ocean move. Sometimes people who die at sea are claimed by Ran.

Váli is the god of vengeance. He's Odin's son. When he was just one day old, he killed Hod.

Vidar is also the god of vengeance and Odin's son. He kills Fenrir the wolf.

THE BIG DEAL ABOUT GIANTS

Giants (also called Jotun) were the first creatures in the universe. They are the sworn enemies of the gods. They're super strong, and many are super ugly. Even though giants tower over gods, giants are far less intelligent, so the gods can usually trick them. There are two kinds of giants—**fire giants** and **frost giants**.

Fire giants live in the unbearable heat of Muspell. Surt is the ruler of the fire giants.

Frost giants live in the frigid mountains of Jotunheim. They're sometimes also called mountain giants. They're big, nasty, and violent. They hate that the gods are cleverer and more magical than they are. Some giants can change shape, and some have beautiful daughters whom the gods marry.

GIANT FACT

GIANTS TURN TO STONE IN THE SUNLIGHT. VIKINGS BELIEVED THAT THE TALL MOUNTAINS OF SCANDINAVIA WERE REALLY GIANTS WHO WERE CAUGHT OUT IN THE SUN. THEY ALSO THOUGHT THAT AVALANCHES WERE CAUSED BY GIANTS SHAKING SNOW FROM THEIR BODIES.

Angrboda is ugly on one side and beautiful on the other. She has three monstrous children with Loki: Fenrir the wolf; Jormungand, the Midgard serpent; and Hel, queen of the dead.

Gerd agreed to become the wife of Frey because she was afraid his servant would put a curse on her to turn her old and ugly.

Thiazi turns himself into an eagle to steal Idunn's apples of youth. Thor kills him. (Thor has no love for frost giants.)

Skadi, Thiazi's daughter, marries Njord and becomes the goddess of skiing and snowshoeing.

Thrym steals Thor's hammer and tries to marry Freya. Thor kills him, too.

Utgard-Loki (also called **Skrymir**) is a trickster giant who rules the castle Utgard. Thor tries to kill him but can't.

FIRE AND ICE—ALIVE!

IN SCANDINAVIA, THE VIKINGS HAD TO ENDURE DEADLY COLD AND BLISTERING HEAT EVERY DAY. THEY BRAVED ICY MOUNTAINS AND HARSH GLACIERS, AS WELL AS FIERY LAVA FROM ACTIVE VOLCANOES. AS A RESULT, THEY VIEWED THE LAND AS SUPERNATURAL. THEY BELIEVED AVALANCHES AND ERUPTING VOLCANOES WERE REALLY FROST AND FIRE GIANTS!

A Few Short Facts About Dwarves and Elves

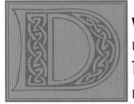**warves** live and work in underground caves in Nidavellir. They are master craftsmen, making magnificent weapons and jewelry that they enhance with magic. Dwarves are very short, very stubborn, and very cunning.

Brokk and **Eitri**—These two brothers created Odin's golden arm ring (Draupnir), Frey's golden boar (Gullinbursti), and Thor's hammer (Mjollnir).

VIKINGS THOUGHT ECHOES WERE THE SOUND OF DWARVES WHISPERING TO ONE ANOTHER.

Sons of Ivaldi—These three dwarves compete against Brokk and Eitri to see who are the best craftsmen. They make Sif's golden hair, Odin's magical spear (Gungnir), and Frey's boat (*Skidbladnir*). Their father is Ivaldi.

Austri, **Vestri**, **Norðri**, and **Suðri** ("East," "West," "North," and "South")—these four strong dwarves hold up the corners of the sky.

SMALL DWARF FACT

IF A DWARF STEPS INTO THE SUNLIGHT, HE'LL TURN TO STONE. SO EVERY TIME YOU SPOT A SMALL STONE ON THE GROUND, IT'S REALLY A DWARF!

Light Elves are bright, glowing creatures. They're closely linked to the Vanir gods. Frey is the ruler of Alfheim, where the Light Elves live. Light Elves have the power to heal and cure sickness. They're barely mentioned in the myths.

Skirnir is Frey's Light Elf servant. He convinces Gerd to marry Frey. In return, Frey gives him his magical sword. He also goes to the dwarves for Odin to get a magic rope strong enough to tie up Fenrir the wolf.

Dark Elves live underground in Svartalfheim. They're brooding creatures that can bring about sickness. Dark Elves are so similar to dwarves that many people believe them to be the same.

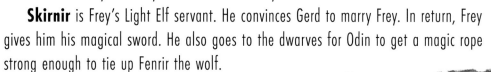

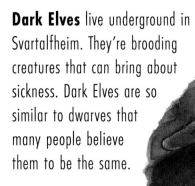

WHAT ABOUT TROLLS?

Trolls live far off in mountain caves, keeping to themselves. They're not friendly, rarely helpful, very strong, and quite stupid. Some people believe that trolls and giants may have been one and the same.

GODS CAN SEE GIANTS, TROLLS, DWARVES, AND ELVES, BUT HUMANS CAN'T.

The Scary Children of Loki and Angrboda

 he trickster Loki has three children with the giantess Angrboda. These children are all so evil and horrible that it's hard to decide which one is truly the worst.

Fenrir is a ferocious wolf who bit off Tyr's hand. He's tied up by a magical rope called **Gleipnir** until Ragnarok comes.

Jormungand (also called the **Midgard serpent**) is a huge, hissing snake who was thrown out of Asgard by Odin. He lives on the ocean floor. His body is so enormous that it circles Midgard, and he bites his own tail. He eats whales for snacks.

IT'S NORSE, OF COURSE!
FENRIR GREYBACK, A WEREWOLF IN THE HARRY POTTER BOOKS, WAS NAMED AFTER FENRIR IN NORSE MYTHOLOGY.

VIKING SAILORS FEARED JORMUNGAND. WHEN HE THRASHED HIS BODY, THE SEAS WOULD GROW ROUGH AND CHURN, CAUSING BOATS TO CAPSIZE AND SAILORS TO DROWN.

GO TO HEL

HEL LIVES IN A GREAT HALL IN NIFLHEIM CALLED **ELJUDNIR**. A WALL OVER A MILE HIGH SURROUNDS THE HALL. GARM, A SNARLING DOG, GUARDS THE MASSIVE GATES. NIDHOGG, A GRUESOME DRAGON WITH HORNS AND BATLIKE WINGS, OFTEN VISITS HEL AND EATS THE FLESH OF THE TRULY WICKED DEAD. WRITHING, HISSING SNAKES COVER THE WALLS OF ELJUDNIR.

INSIDE ELJUDNIR, HEL HAS MANY SERVANTS. THEY MOVE SO SLOWLY, IT'S DIFFICULT TO TELL IF THEY'RE MOVING AT ALL. HEL IS GREEDY, ALWAYS DESIRING MORE PEOPLE TO BE BROUGHT DOWN TO SERVE HER. HER PLATE IS NAMED HUNGER. HER KNIFE IS NAMED FAMINE. HER BED IS NAMED SICKBED.

Hel is the queen of Niflheim, the underworld. Half of her body is alive, young, and pretty, and the other half is dead, old, and rotting.

IT'S NORSE, OF COURSE! IN NORSE MYTHOLOGY, TO "GO TO HEL" MEANS TO DIE.

The War Between the Gods
(Or How Odin Lost His Eye and Mimir Lost His Head)

din, father of the Aesir and creator of humans, had questions about the universe. Lots and lots of questions. He wanted to know everything about everything. But where would he find the great wisdom to learn the answers?

Odin journeyed far into Jotunheim, land of the frost giants, where Mimir's Well bubbled. One thick root of Yggdrasil, the World Tree, was fed by this magical well. The wise giant Mimir cared for the well. Mimir was also the god of memory.

Odin greeted him. "Please, Mimir, may I have a drink from your waters?"

Mimir shook his head. Only he was allowed to drink from his well of knowledge. It held the secrets of all nine worlds.

"Just one drink?" Odin pleaded. "I'll give anything for a sip."

"Anything?" asked Mimir. "I want your eye."

Odin started to say no. Then he thought about it. What good was his eye when he couldn't understand all he saw? Besides, he had two eyes.

Odin plucked out one of his eyes and plopped it into the well. Then he filled the horn called Gjallerhorn with the magic water. Odin drank it down. Cool water—and wisdom—flowed through his body. Odin now understood the universe.

But Odin wanted more knowledge. For this, he would need to learn the secret of the runes, mysterious written symbols. No god understood what the runes meant.

Odin went to Yggdrasil. The tall ash reached up to the splendor of Asgard and down to the darkness of Niflheim. Great wisdom lay within the tree. Odin thrust his spear through his body, pinning himself to the wide trunk.

Odin hung from the tree for nine long days and nine long nights. He was cold, hungry, and in terrible agony, but he stayed on the tree. Gaining true wisdom required determination and pain. On the ninth night, Odin was close to death. Weak and dizzy, he looked down and saw mysterious letters on the tree's roots. These were the runes. The letters swirled, and their meaning suddenly became clear to him. He now knew the secrets of nature. He could cure sickness, direct the lost, calm a storm, speak to the dead, and see the future.

Odin returned to Asgard filled with supreme wisdom. Sitting high on his throne, he looked over the great halls that glittered with brilliant gold. His children, the Aesir, lived in peace and harmony, and all was good.

However, the Vanir did not think all was good. They lived in Vanaheim and were jealous of the brilliant glow of Asgard. They wanted gold, too. They sent the witch Gullveig to bring back riches for them.

Gullveig swept into Asgard and stood before the All-Father. "Give me gold—now!" she demanded.

Odin did not like her greedy attitude, so he had her tossed into a big fire. But Gullveig walked out of the fire completely unharmed. She was a witch, after all.

"Where's the gold?" the Vanir asked when she returned to Vanaheim.

Gullveig told them what Odin had tried to do to her. The Vanir were angry. They declared war on the Aesir. Spells were cast. Walls crumbled. Battles raged on and on.

With powerful gods fighting powerful gods, wise Odin knew that the war would only end with all the gods killing one another. He visited Njord, the ruler of the Vanir.

"We must declare a truce," Odin told him.

Njord agreed. "But how can we be sure that both sides will stop fighting?"

They decided to trade two gods each to keep the peace. The two best Vanir—Njord and his son, Frey—would come live with the Aesir in Asgard.

"I'm going, too," declared the goddess Freya. She refused to be left behind, so she went with her

father and twin brother. The Aesir were honored to get such an amazing goddess in the deal.

Odin chose handsome Hoenir and wise Mimir to live with the Vanir in Vanaheim. Hoenir became the Vanir's new leader. He made many clever decisions with Mimir by his side. The trade seemed fair, and peace settled on the two lands.

Until one afternoon when Hoenir was fixing his hair. He was proud of his thick hair.

The Vanir called an emergency meeting. Hoenir searched for Mimir. Where was he? But Mimir was out in the countryside. Hoenir tried to stall, but the Vanir

READING RUNES

RUNES WERE WRITINGS USED BY THE VIKINGS. THEY WERE CARVED INTO WOOD OR STONE, SO ALL THE LETTERS AND SYMBOLS HAD STRAIGHT LINES. THE VIKINGS BELIEVED THAT EACH LETTER HAD MAGICAL POWERS. CAN YOU WRITE YOUR NAME IN RUNES?

A B C D E F G H

IJ K L M N O P Q

R S T UVW X Y Z

Mimir's head told Odin not to take revenge on the Vanir. A war between the gods would end in destruction. Odin listened to Mimir's head, and he went to Hoenir. Together they agreed that there would be no more fighting among the gods.

Odin brought Mimir's head to the well beneath Yggdrasil. He floated it alongside his eye, and the waters of knowledge kept it safe. In the days to come, it would whisper many secrets to Odin.

wanted their leader's advice right away. Without Mimir whispering in his ear, Hoenir couldn't make a decision. He had nothing wise to say at all. It soon became clear that although Hoenir looked good, he was lacking in the brains department.

The Vanir were angry once more. The Aesir had tricked them into giving away Njord, their great ruler, for this fool! What did they do? They cut off Mimir's head and sent it to Odin!

Odin was incredibly upset. Poor Mimir had done nothing wrong. Odin cradled Mimir's head and sang to it, magically giving it back the power of speech. He rubbed it with herbs so it would never rot. From then on, Mimir's head told its wisdom only to Odin.

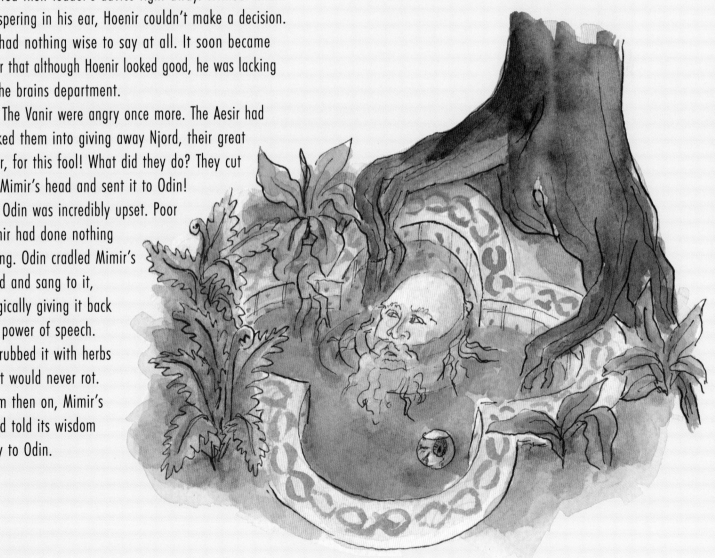

TREASURES OF THE GODS
(OR HOW SIF LOST HER HAIR)

All the gods and goddesses in Asgard agreed that the goddess Sif had the best hair ever. Her silky yellow-gold tresses rippled like a waterfall down her back. First thing every morning, Sif brushed her golden mane with one thousand strokes, causing each strand to shine brighter than the sun on a hot summer's day.

One morning, Sif began to brush, and the bristles scraped bare skin. She let out a blood-curdling scream. Her husband, Thor, raced to her side and gasped in horror. Sif's golden hair had been chopped off while she'd slept. She was completely bald!

Sif felt her bare scalp with her fingertips. "Who did this to me?" she wailed.

"Loki," Thor, god of thunder, growled. "It must have been Loki. Trouble is always caused by Loki."

Thor stomped off to find Loki, god of mischief. When he spotted the trickster, Thor raised his large fist. "You did this to her."

"Me? Do what? To who?" Loki lied, backing away. "I haven't done anything."

"Oh, really?" Thor narrowed his blue eyes. "Sif's hair was so pretty, and now it's . . . it's . . ." Thor fumbled for the words.

"Gone?" Loki filled in. "Hacked off?"

"Exactly!" Thor's face grew redder than his fiery hair. "I knew it was you."

"It was only a joke. You know, funny." Loki forced a hearty laugh.

"Not funny!" roared Thor. "My wife is bald. I will pound you!"

"No need for violence." Loki nervously held up his hands. "I can fix this. I'll get Sif's hair back—even more beautiful than before. I'll replace her hair with hair made of real gold. How's that?"

Thor lowered his fist. "Fine. But if you don't, I will finish you."

Loki hurried to Nidavellir, the underground land of the dwarves. He made his way down long, winding tunnels, searching for the workshop of Brokk and Eitri. They were said to be the most skilled craftsmen in all of the nine worlds. If anyone could spin hair out of gold, it would be these two dwarves.

"Hello, there." Loki poked his head into a cave and saw three dwarves. He gave them his widest smile. "I come from Asgard in search of Brokk and Eitri to do important work for the gods. Are you them?"

"Absolutely not," said one dwarf. "We are the sons of Ivaldi. We're the most talented craftsmen around. Anything Brokk and Eitri can build, we can build better."

"You don't say." Loki began to scheme. "I've been sent on a very important mission to find three amazing gifts worthy of the gods. Are you up to it?"

"We are up to it," said the second son of Ivaldi. "Let us do it. Please?"

Loki scratched his head, as if thinking over the matter. "I guess I could give you boys a shot. I know . . . how about a contest against Brokk and Eitri? Three gifts for the gods. The best gift wins."

"Bring it on," said the third son of Ivaldi. "Name your gifts."

Loki told them they could create two gifts of their own choosing. "But the third must be hair. Thor's wife is missing all her golden hair. So very strange and sad, but I'm trying to help her. I do that, you know? How about making hair spun of real gold?"

Loki left the sons of Ivaldi and found the cave of Brokk and Eitri.

"Well, hello there!" he called. "I've come from the gods of the Aesir. I've been told by the sons of Ivaldi that their work is superior to yours."

"Oh, please," scoffed Brokk. "Those boys can't twist a pipe cleaner."

"Can't cut a snowflake out of paper," added Eitri.

"That's not how they tell it. In fact"—Loki lowered his voice—"they've challenged you to a contest."

"What kind of contest?" asked Eitri.

"Three treasures worthy of the gods. The best gift wins, and the winning dwarves claim the title of Best Craftsmen." Loki had a plan. He'd use gifts made by these two talented dwarves to get the gods on his side. If Thor stayed angry, he'd bring Odin into it and Loki would need all the help he could get.

Brokk knew not to trust the trickster. "We pass."

"Oh, I see. You're scared." Loki's voice dripped with fake understanding. "Well, if you feel you're not up to it. . . ."

"Not up to it? As if!" cried Eitri. "We will battle the sons of Ivaldi for the title, but on one condition. If we win, we get your head."

"Excuse me?" Loki was startled.

"If the gods choose one of our gifts as the best, we cut off your head. Deal?"

"Fine, but only my head," said Loki. "No hurting any other part of my body."

Loki would make sure that Brokk and Eitri lost the contest. Then the gods would get amazing gifts, Sif would get her hair, and he'd still have his head. *That won't be hard for someone as cunning as me*, he thought.

Brokk and Eitri got to work. Eitri was a magnificent craftsman. Brokk pumped his bellows to keep the furnace flames burning bright, so Eitri could twist and mold metal into fabulous treasures. The air from the bellows fanned the fire, making the flames dance.

"Don't stop pumping no matter what," Eitri warned his brother. If Brokk stopped, the flames would die out and the metal wouldn't stretch.

Eitri threw an old pig skin into the fire. It crackled and sparked. "Keep it hot, Brokk," he said.

A fly buzzed around Brokk's ear. Brokk shook his head, trying to shoo it away. The fly buzzed louder and louder.

Brokk didn't know the fly was really Loki. Loki had the power to shapeshift, and he'd turned himself into a fly.

Brokk wished he could swat the pesky fly, but he didn't dare take his hands off the bellows. The fly kept buzzing.

Brokk blew on the fly. The fly would not go away. He spit at the fly. The fly would not go away. Then the fly bit Brokk's hand!

Brokk cried out in pain, but he never stopped pumping the bellows. Eitri reached into the furnace and pulled out a large boar with shiny gold bristles.

"Well done, bro!" called Brokk.

"Keep it hot," Eitri told his brother. He threw a lump of gold into the fire.

Loki the Fly began to panic. He couldn't let these dwarves make another fabulous gift. He bit Brokk's neck—hard.

"Ow!" howled Brokk—but he still didn't stop pumping. Eitri shaped the lump of gold. He transformed it into a thick, golden arm ring.

Loki the Fly gasped. The gods would love these gifts, and he would surely lose his head.

No more Mr. Nice Fly, he told himself, as Eitri placed a piece of iron in the fire.

Loki the Fly zoomed full speed toward Brokk and bit his eyelids.

Brokk shuddered in agony. He whipped his head back and forth, trying to fling off the vicious fly. Loki the Fly held on, biting again and again. Brokk's eyelids swelled. Tears streamed down his cheeks. He could barely see.

"Don't slack off, brother! Keep up the pace!" called Eitri.

Brokk groaned and made himself pump faster.

Finally, Eitri pulled the iron from the fire. From it, he'd made an enormous silver hammer.

"The handle's too short. It needed more heat," he grumbled to Brokk. Then he looked over at him. "What's with your eyes?"

"A pest did it," said Brokk, as he saw the fly dart behind a big rock and change back into Loki.

"I need a nap." Eitri yawned. "You take these gifts to the gods in Asgard, and then cut off Loki's head."

"Gladly," said Brokk.

In Asgard, Loki brought Brokk and the three sons of Ivaldi into Gladsheim, Odin's golden hall. Odin sat on his throne. Next to him sat Thor and Frey, god of the harvest. They would be the judges.

"You must choose whose gifts are better, the three gifts made by the sons of Ivaldi or the three gifts made by Brokk and Eitri," Loki told them.

The first son of Ivaldi stepped forward with a pile of golden hair. "This hair is spun from real gold. It will magically attach to Sif's head and grow there forever, long and beautiful."

Sif placed the hair on her bald head. Instantly, the hair became one with her scalp. The golden tresses flowed down her back and radiated more sunshine than ever before. Sif smiled. "I like it."

"Good job!" boomed Thor.

The second son of Ivaldi stepped toward Odin. "I present to you with the magical spear called Gungnir. This spear will always hit its target. Try it out. Throw it at the smudge of dirt on the door at the far end of the hall."

Odin squinted his one eye. "I can't see any smudge." He threw the spear anyway.

The spear hit the smudge. The gods cheered.

"Impressive," said Odin.

"For Frey, I have this." The third son of Ivaldi pulled a tightly folded paper from a pouch. "When unfolded, this little paper becomes a huge boat called *Skidbladnir*. It is sturdy enough to hold one hundred gods. It will always sail in fair winds. And you can fold it up and carry it with you."

Frey beamed. "It's incredible!"

Loki let out his breath. *These are three amazing gifts. I don't need to worry. One is sure to win. My head will be just fine.*

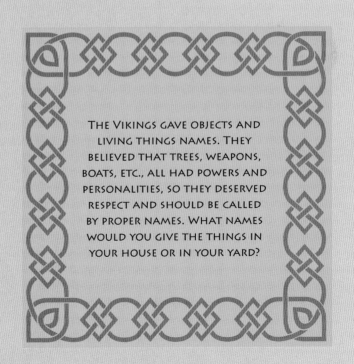

THE VIKINGS GAVE OBJECTS AND LIVING THINGS NAMES. THEY BELIEVED THAT TREES, WEAPONS, BOATS, ETC., ALL HAD POWERS AND PERSONALITIES, SO THEY DESERVED RESPECT AND SHOULD BE CALLED BY PROPER NAMES. WHAT NAMES WOULD YOU GIVE THE THINGS IN YOUR HOUSE OR IN YOUR YARD?

Odin turned to Brokk, whose eyes were still swollen. "What did you bring us?"

"My brother and I made this arm ring for you. It is called Draupnir." Brokk handed the All-Father the solid-gold arm ring.

Odin tested its weight. "Why is it so heavy?"

"Because every ninth night, the ring will drip eight times and create eight more gold rings of the same weight," said the dwarf.

Odin—who never grinned—grinned.

Brokk turned to Frey. "I present you with Gullinbursti, the boar with the golden bristles. He will pull your chariot as fast as the wind and light the darkness, so you can always find your way."

Then Brokk handed the silver hammer to Thor. "This is Mjollnir. It is the most powerful hammer ever. It can never be broken, and it will always return to your hand."

Thor inspected it. "Handle's too short."

Brokk hung his head. "That's my fault."

Loki smirked.

The gods huddled together and chose . . . Thor's hammer as the winner! It didn't matter that the handle was short. With the mighty hammer, Thor could keep Asgard safe from giants and trolls. Brokk and Eitri were named Best Craftsmen.

"Wait, no!" cried Loki. "Thor, what about Sif's hair? Isn't it better than a hammer with a short handle?"

"Sif's hair is pretty," agreed Thor. "But my hammer will never miss its target and can grow and shrink to the size I want it to be. How cool is that?"

Brokk stepped up to Loki. "Your head, please. We had a deal."

Loki gulped. This had not gone as planned. He tried to make a run for it.

Thor caught him. "Cut off his head now," he said, handing the trickster to Brokk.

"Not so fast," said Loki. "Our deal was that you can have my head, but you can't hurt any other part of me. That means you can't touch my neck."

There was no way to take Loki's head off his body without harming his neck. Loki had tricked them!

Brokk let Loki go.

In the end, Sif got back her golden hair, and the gods received their most prized treasures—all because of Loki's tricks.

The Walls of Asgard
(Or Tale of an Eight-Legged Horse)

Thor was away fighting trolls to the east, and the Aesir were worried. The wall around Asgard had been destroyed during the battle between the Aesir and the Vanir. Without a wall and without Thor, they were unprotected from frost giants and trolls. Even with their magic, the gods couldn't build a strong enough wall. So when a stranger appeared in Asgard and said he was a master builder, they listened.

"I can build a stone wall so tall and so thick that no one will get through," he bragged. "And I can do it fast. I'll finish in a year and a half."

The gods raised their eyebrows at one another. The builder's offer seemed too good to be true.

"How much gold do you want for your work?" asked Odin.

The builder rubbed the shiny gray coat of the magnificent stallion he'd ridden in on and shook his head. "No gold."

"What, then?" asked Loki. Loki was always on the lookout for other tricksters.

"Three things, that's all," said the builder. "I would like the goddess Freya to be my wife. I would like the sun, and I would like the moon."

"No way!" cried Frey, brother of Freya.

Odin stroked his long beard. "We need to talk about this. Would you wait over there?" He pointed the builder to a nearby stream, then gathered the gods.

"What's to talk about?" demanded Frey when the builder left. "He's beneath her."

"I'll say. There's no way I'm marrying that guy." Freya, goddess of love and beauty, put her hands on her hips. Her red-gold hair was braided in a crown. "Don't even think you can sell me like that."

"Also, we can't give up the sun and the moon." Balder, god of light, raised his fair face to the sky.

"Let's forget it," said Heimdall, the watchman. "The builder's price is too high."

"True," said Odin. "We will find another way—"

"Hold up." Loki stepped forward. "You're all being too hasty. Let's think about this. This stranger offers to build a high, thick stone wall surrounding Asgard in only eighteen months. Impossible! It can't be done."

"What are you saying?" asked Balder.

Loki sighed. *Why couldn't these gods keep up with his superior logic?* "I'm saying that we will win. Freya will not have to marry him, and the sun and the moon will stay in the sky where they belong. The stranger will build us a good part of the wall for free, but then time will run out. We will shoo him out of Asgard, and someone else can finish the wall."

"What if he can build the wall?" Freya narrowed her eyes at Loki.

"Nonsense!" Loki turned away from Freya's icy glare. "We'll make it harder. He will only get six months, and he can't have any help building the wall."

All the gods, except Freya, liked Loki's plan. They thought it quite clever. Odin called the builder over and told him the terms.

He agreed. "But only if my stallion, Svadilfari, can help me carry the rocks."

"A horse? Of course." Loki didn't think one horse would make a difference.

Odin and the builder shook hands on the deal.

The next day, gray clouds blanketed the winter sky and a frigid wind howled, but the builder worked with unstoppable energy. He traveled deep into the mountains, and his strong horse hauled back boulder after boulder. The builder worked with the strength of a giant. Svadilfari carried massive weights of stone without stopping for a rest or a drink of water.

The gods watched in amazement. *Could the horse be magical?* they wondered.

The builder stacked each boulder tightly. Stone after stone. The builder and his horse worked night and day without sleep. They worked through blizzards and ice storms. The wall grew taller and taller.

Three days before the end of winter, Odin grimly gathered the gods around his throne. "The wall is nearly done. He has only a small part to finish. I fear we may lose Freya, the sun, and the moon."

Freya pointed at Loki. "This is all your fault!"

"Loki thinks he's so clever, but he always brings trouble." Frey wrapped his arm around his sister. "Without dear Freya, we will be lost. She brings light to Asgard."

"Without the sun and the moon in the sky, we will all live in darkness," added Balder.

"Loki must be punished," said Heimdall.

"I say we send for Thor." Freya seethed with anger. "He'll punish Loki with his hammer."

"Whoa! Let's not get ahead of ourselves. There's still time. I'll make sure that wall is never finished." Loki definitely did not want Thor involved.

"How will you do that?" demanded Odin.

"Just leave the details to me." Loki walked off confidently, as if he had a great plan. In truth, he had no idea what to do. But he'd figure it out. He always did.

Loki sat under a pine tree and watched the builder and his stallion work. Svadilfari dragged each massive stone down from the mountain with unwavering focus.

That night as the full moon rose, a black mare appeared by the pine tree. The builder and Svadilfari were heading back to the mountain for more stone. The mare whinnied, and Svadilfari's ears pricked up. She whinnied again. Svadilfari turned his head in her direction.

Then the mare galloped off, kicking up fresh snow on the frozen field. Svadilfari watched in wonder. This horse was beautiful! She whinnied once more, and Svadilfari chased after her.

"No! Stop!" called the builder.

Svadilfari didn't stop. He galloped faster, his eyes on the mare. The mare ran into the forest, and Svadilfari followed. The builder lumbered to keep up, shouting all the while, but soon he lost sight of his stallion.

He searched all night. But his horse was gone.

The sun rose, and the builder had no choice but to work alone. He could only drag one stone from the mountain in the time Svadilfari had dragged ten. He worked all day and the next night, collapsing with exhaustion. Without his stallion, he'd never finish the wall in time.

"I've been tricked!" he bellowed. The builder looked about for someone to blame, but he was all alone. The gods sat around cozy fires inside their halls. His anger bloomed into a rage—and his body swelled into that of a gruesome giant.

"*Grrr!* I will destroy this wall! I will destroy you all!" he cried.

Luckily, at that very moment, Thor was on his way home. He heard the giant's roar and rushed back to Asgard. He raised his mighty hammer and smashed the giant on the head. The giant dropped dead.

The gods raced outside and let up a cheer. "Freya, the sun, and the moon are saved!"

"Good work, Thor," said Odin.

Freya looked around. "Not that I care, but where's Loki?"

The trickster was nowhere in sight. In fact, he stayed missing for several months.

Then one day, Loki returned to Asgard. He led a colt with a shiny silver-gray coat. The baby horse looked very much like Svadilfari, except it had eight legs—four in the front and four in the back. The eight-legged horse could fly through the sky and gallop through the ocean's waves. He was faster than any other horse.

Loki gave this magnificent horse to Odin, and Odin named him Sleipnir.

Loki stood to the side and waited for someone to thank him for saving Asgard from the horrible giant. He waited and waited. No one ever thanked him.

Did they know that Loki had shape-shifted, and he had been the black mare?

Loki's Children
(or How Tyr Lost His Hand)

"Beware!" the three Norns called to Odin one day, as he walked by the Well of Urd. Odin stopped and paid close attention. The Norns were powerful giantesses who wove each god's and human's fate in their tapestry of life. They decided what would become of everyone.

"Tell me more," said Odin.

"Beware of the trickster Loki's young children. When the end comes, as it will, Loki's children will cause the death of you and all the gods," said the Norns.

Odin thought of the three hideous children Loki had just had with the giantess Angrboda: Fenrir, a wolf; Jormungand, a sea serpent; and Hel, who was half beautiful girl and half rotting corpse. He shuddered. He'd get them out of Asgard immediately.

First, Odin grabbed Jormungand, who spat venom from his fangs. Odin hurled him into the deep gray sea surrounding Midgard. When the snake hit the water, he began to grow. He grew and grew. Soon the serpent was so enormous that his body wrapped completely around the land of the humans.

Then Odin turned to Loki's daughter, Hel, who glowered at him. Decaying flesh hung from one side of her face. Her other cheek was smooth and rosy. Odin banished the girl to the darkness of Niflheim, granting her rule over the frozen realm of the dead. Down in the gloom, she'd receive those who'd died from an accident, sickness, or old age. Heroes who died in battle would be sent to Odin's own hall, Valhalla, in Asgard.

Finally, Odin turned to Fenrir. He was only a small wolf cub. What harm could he do? Odin allowed Fenrir to stay in Asgard.

But as the days passed, Fenrir's body grew larger. His fangs grew longer. His claws grew sharper. His growl grew louder. And he became meaner and meaner. Soon he was a gigantic, snarling, ferocious beast.

"Please, do something," the gods pleaded to Odin. "This savage wolf will hurt us all."

Odin went to Loki. He told him to tie up Fenrir.

Loki laughed. "Forget it. I'd never do that to my own son."

But Loki wasn't telling the truth. That wasn't the real reason. Loki was as afraid of Fenrir as the gods were.

"Any volunteers to tie up the wolf?" Odin asked the gods gathered around his throne.

No one raised a hand. It was too dangerous a task, even for the gods.

Odin decided to trick Fenrir. He called the wolf to him.

"This is the strongest chain in Asgard." Odin held up a thick iron chain. "It is so incredibly strong that I bet even your strength is no match for it."

"Oh, please!" Fenrir was proud of how strong he'd grown. "I am tougher than your chain. Wrap it around me. Go on!"

He let them bind him with the heavy chain. The gods grinned. How easy! The dumb wolf had pretty much tied himself up.

Bam! Fenrir arched his back and busted the chain into bits.

Quickly, Odin found another chain, twice as thick and twice as heavy as the first one. Fenrir allowed himself to be tied up again. This time the gods wrapped the chain tighter. They made a bigger knot.

Bam! Fenrir shattered this chain, too.

The gods huddled around Odin. "What should we do now?"

"We need magic to contain him." Odin instructed Skirnir, a Light Elf who was Frey's messenger, to visit the dwarves and ask them to craft the strongest chain ever.

Skirnir traveled to Nidavellir, where the dwarves had their underground workshops. The dwarves could forge the most amazing treasures from metals and ores. When Skirnir returned, he presented Odin with a thin silk ribbon.

"What's this?" Odin was surprised. "It's so flimsy."

"The dwarves call it Gleipnir," said Skirnir. "It was braided from the noise of a cat's paws, the breath of a fish, the beard of a young woman, the saliva of a bird, the roots of a mountain, and the sinews of a bear. They say Gleipnir is unbreakable."

Odin called over Fenrir. "May I test your strength one more time?"

"Test away." Drool dripped from Fenrir's glistening fangs. "I will break all your chains, All-Father."

Then Fenrir saw the ribbon. Instantly, he was suspicious. "I'm not going up against dwarf magic."

"Wait," said Odin. "If this magic thread does bind you, then we have no cause to fear you and we'll let you go free."

"Free? Really?" Fenrir thought about it. "I'll agree to let you tie me up with that magic ribbon only if one

of you puts his hand in my mouth while you do. This way you can't go back on your word."

All the Aesir stared at Fenrir's long, pointy fangs. No one spoke.

Tyr, the bravest of all the gods, stepped forward. He placed his right hand inside the snarling wolf's mouth. Odin wrapped the ribbon around the wolf's hairy body. He tied it around all four feet. He knotted it tightly to a large rock.

"Let's do this," said Tyr.

Fenrir arched his back. He thrashed from side to side. His eyes bulged as he fought to get free. The more he struggled, the tighter the ribbon grew. It would not break.

Fenrir grew tired. "Your magic ribbon won. Now let me go."

But Odin and the gods refused to untie him.

Fenrir was angry. He'd been tricked, and now he'd be tied up forever. Growling and foaming at the mouth, he snapped his jaws shut—and bit off Tyr's hand!

Tyr howled. His right hand was gone!

He'd have to learn to hold his sword with his left hand.

The gods kept Fenrir tied up. They left him in a swamp. There he will stay until the end of the world, when he'll finally break free . . . and go after Odin for a promise never kept.

Idunn and the Magic Apples
(or The Great Eagle and Falcon Chase)

he goddess Idunn lived in a beautiful garden in Asgard. In her garden, flowers always bloomed, giving off the sweetest perfume. The ripest fruit hung from the trees, and the grass grew green and lush. Nothing ever withered or died in Idunn's garden.

Idunn was as sweet as her fruit, and the gods visited her garden for the magic apples she kept in a golden box. Eating one apple kept a god young. But, after a time, the apple's magic wore off. The god's bones would begin to ache, and his skin would wrinkle. So he'd return to Idunn for another apple, and he'd be young again.

One time, Odin, Loki, and Hoenir, an old god who'd once been traded to the Vanir to keep the peace, were journeying through Midgard. They had traveled across the wide deserts and tall mountains that bordered Jotunheim, land of the frost giants. They'd grown weary and hungry.

"Time to eat, Loki," said Odin.

Loki looked inside his pack and gulped. *Oh, no!* He'd forgotten to pack food for their journey. Loki was never very dependable when it came to practical things. But he was quick to invent solutions.

"Look there." Loki pointed to the valley, where a herd of cattle grazed. "Fresh meat is really the way to go."

Loki caught an ox and roasted its meat over an open fire. Odin and Hoenir waited eagerly to take a bite.

Loki tested the meat. It was raw. He kept it over the fire to cook longer.

Loki tested it again. And again. The meat hadn't roasted at all. *What's going on?* wondered Loki. Annoyed, he inspected the fire, but the flames burned high and bright.

"Is this one of your tricks?" demanded Odin.

"Why would you say that? I don't know what's wrong—" began Loki.

"I know." An enormous eagle perched atop the tallest pine tree interrupted them. "I used magic to make sure that ox would never cook in your fire. I will fix your fire, if you share your meat with me. I eat first, then you eat."

The gods agreed.

The huge bird blew magic on the fire. The flames crackled and roasted the ox. Then the eagle swooped down and greedily gobbled the best parts of the meat.

"Hey, that's not sharing!" Loki grabbed his spear and tried to smack the eagle away. His spear stuck into the eagle's side. The eagle glared at Loki and flapped his large wings. It rose into the air—dragging the spear and Loki with him!

Loki couldn't let go. Magic had glued his hands to his spear!

The eagle flew close to the ground. He banged Loki against jagged rocks, through prickly bushes, and under cold river water.

"Ow! Let me go!" cried Loki. "Please, stop!"

"I will only stop if you promise to bring Idunn and her apples to me in the forest," said the eagle.

Loki knew Idunn never left her garden in Asgard. He knew no one besides gods was permitted to eat the apples of youth. But, bruised and battered, Loki only cared about saving himself.

"You got it," he told the eagle.

The eagle pulled the spear from his side, and Loki tumbled to the ground.

Loki limped back to Odin and Hoenir, who'd finished the meat without him. He told them about the eagle, naturally leaving out the part about Idunn and the apples. They laughed. Imagine being carried away by an eagle!

Loki didn't find it funny. Not at all. He hadn't planned on keeping his promise to the eagle . . . until now.

The next day, Loki went to Idunn's garden. "Hello, there," he called to the goddess. "You look awfully pretty. An apple a day and all that. I could use an apple myself."

"Really?" Idunn kept track of who was in need of one of her apples. "You're looking good."

"I try." Loki ran his fingers through his thick, dark hair. "Feeling a bit tired, though. Run down."

Idunn gave him a magic apple. Loki ate it, the juices running down his chin.

"So the strangest thing happened." Loki leaned against her apple tree. "I was walking in the forest, and I saw a tree with apples just like yours."

"That can't be," said Idunn. "My magic apples are one of a kind."

"I fear you may be wrong. These may even be better." Loki shook his head, pretending to be dismayed.

"Impossible," said Idunn.

"I know, right? You be the judge." Loki reached for her hand. "Let me show you. It won't take long. Oh, and bring your golden box of apples so we can compare."

Idunn was curious, so she let Loki lead her out of Asgard. They crossed the Bifrost, the rainbow bridge, and entered the forests of Midgard. As they walked, the trees grew tall and thick, blocking the sun.

Idunn searched for an apple tree, but all she saw were pine trees. "I think we should turn back."

At that moment, an enormous eagle swooped down from the tallest tree. It grabbed Idunn and her golden box in its claws. Idunn screamed.

"I am not really an eagle," said the great bird. "I am the giant Thiazi in disguise. I've come to take you and your apples to my great hall in the mountains of Jotunheim."

And with that, he carried them away.

"A giant? Well, that explains a lot," Loki muttered.

Over the next few days, the gods in Asgard felt the effects of age for the first time. Thor's back ached. Freya's hair turned gray. Frey shuffled when he walked. Heimdall had trouble hearing. They all took naps.

The gods visited Idunn's garden for an apple. Flowers no longer bloomed here. The plants had turned brown. "Where's Idunn?" they asked.

Bragi, god of poetry, didn't know what had become of his wife. He wanted to search for Idunn, but he didn't have the energy. He'd grown too old.

Odin called a meeting of the frail and feeble gods. Odin's one eye had turned cloudy, yet he still looked at Loki suspiciously. Loki looked awfully young and healthy. Of course, Odin didn't know that Loki had been the last to eat a magic apple. But Odin did know that if there was trouble, Loki was involved.

"Where is Idunn?" Odin demanded.

"Her? Well, it's like this . . ." Loki stalled.

With an aching back and a shaky old-man grip, Thor raised his mighty hammer. "Spill it, Loki."

"I saw Thiazi take her. You know, the giant? He's holding her prisoner in his hall high in the mountains," confessed Loki.

"And you just let him take her?" croaked Thor. "I will pound you!"

"No need. I will get her back. Quick, quick, you'll see," promised Loki.

Loki thought fast. How would he do this? The giant was way bigger and stronger than he was. Plus, Idunn was on top of a high mountain, and that would take forever to climb.

"Freya, lend me your falcon-feather cloak," said Loki.

Freya started to protest, but she had trouble remembering what she'd meant to say. She handed Loki the cloak.

Loki wrapped it around his shoulders and flew to the land of the giants. He flew through the highest window in Thiazi's hall. Idunn sat in a corner of the room, her arms wrapped around her knees. The box of apples sat by her side. Thiazi had gone to the sea to fish, but he'd return soon.

Loki used magic and turned Idunn into a nut. Grabbing the nut, he soared through the sky.

At the same time, Thiazi walked up the mountain path toward his castle. He looked into the air and saw the shiny black wings of a falcon. He knew it was Loki.

Thiazi turned himself back into an eagle. He soared after the falcon. Loki flew fast. Thiazi flew faster. The eagle gained on the falcon.

From his throne in Asgard, Odin watched the chase. He instructed the gods to stack a huge pile of wood near the walls of Asgard.

"Here comes Loki," called Heimdall, watchman of the gods.

Loki the Falcon flew over the wall, entering Asgard.

"Here comes Thiazi," called Heimdall. "Light the fire!"

The gods set fire to the wood pile and it burst into flames as Thiazi crossed over the wall. The flames ignited his wings. Thiazi tumbled to the ground. Thor waited with his mighty hammer. He pounded the giant, killing him.

Loki used magic and turned the nut back into Idunn and her apples. She quickly handed each of the gods an apple, and they became young once more. Even Loki got an apple—because Idunn was still as sweet as her fruit.

Revenge of the Giant's Daughter
(or The God with the Nice Feet)

nside a cave in the steep Jotunheim mountainside, the giantess Skadi poked the fire and wondered what was keeping her father. She peered out over the land, searching for his hulking figure. All she saw was an eagle chasing a falcon in the sky. Something was wrong. Thiazi was never late for dinner. Especially when they were having goat.

Days went by, and her father didn't return. Skadi finally learned that Thiazi had been killed by the gods. At first, she wept. Then she grew angry. She strapped on her helmet and grabbed her sword and shield. She headed to Asgard to avenge her father.

Heimdall, watchman of the gods, let out a cry of alarm as Skadi crossed the icy waters of the River Ifing.

Thor appeared with his magic hammer in his hand.

"Move out of my way!" Skadi tried to push past the red-bearded god.

"Hardly!" Thor raised his hammer.

"Wait, Thor!" From his throne in his hall, Odin had seen Skadi enter Asgard. Now he hurried toward them. "Let's hear what she has to say."

"You killed my father." Skadi bravely stared Odin in his one eye. "I'm sure you can kill me, too. I don't care. I am ready to die to bring honor to Thiazi's name." She jabbed her sword at him.

"Stop that." Odin caught the blade in his hand. "We will not kill or hurt you."

"We won't?" asked Thor. He liked nothing more than pounding giants.

"No. I feel bad that I killed her father, and I respect her courage," Odin told Thor. He turned to Skadi. "What would you like from me?"

"Can you bring my father back to life?" she asked hopefully.

"I cannot," he said. "How about a gift of gold?"

Skadi shook her head. What would she do with gold? She lived a simple life in the mountains. She sighed. She was lonely now without her father.

That gave her an idea.

"I would like a husband," said Skadi. "A kind, noble god with a good sense of humor."

Skadi looked at the gods who'd gathered around. Her gaze landed on Balder. Balder's wavy golden hair gleamed in the sunlight, and his honey-brown eyes twinkled. From his square jaw to his smooth skin, Balder was the best-looking god. Skadi wanted to marry him.

Of course, Odin knew what she was thinking. (He knew most everything.) So Odin added a twist. "I will grant you a god for a husband, but you must choose him by his feet. The gods' bodies and faces will be covered. All you will be able to see is their feet."

Skadi's heart fluttered as she gazed upon gorgeous Balder. A god this amazing-looking definitely had to have amazing-looking feet. Choosing him would be easy.

The gods lined up behind a long tapestry. Skadi walked by, inspecting their bare feet.

Hairy big toes = no

Bumpy knuckles = no

Toe fungus = no

Extra toe = no

Sweaty cheese smell = definitely no

She stopped in front of the final pair of feet. The skin was softer than a baby's. Each toe and toenail was perfectly shaped. And they smelled like melted butter!

These feet must belong to Balder, thought Skadi. And now beautiful Balder would belong to her. She chose those feet.

The god showed himself, and Skadi gasped. The gorgeous feet did not belong to Balder. (His had the bumpy knuckles!). They belonged to old Njord, father of Frey and Freya!

Njord was a Vanir god who'd been traded to the Aesir in the early days to keep the peace. He was god of the seas. Njord's skin was chapped and weathered. His scraggly gray beard was caked with salt, his back was bent, and his hands smelled like fish.

Skadi was not happy. At all.

Because she'd made a deal with Odin, she married Njord. She became the goddess of winter and skiing. Over time, Skadi discovered Njord was kind and noble, and told hysterical jokes. Everything she'd wanted in a husband.

And he had nice feet that smelled like butter.

The only problem the happy couple had was where to live. Skadi hated the salty sea air and the scratchy sand. The seagulls' high-pitched screams made her want to tear out her hair. Njord hated the frigid mountain winds and the icy, narrow pathways of Skadi's homeland. The wolves' mournful howls gave him the shivers.

What did they do? They spent nine days at the sea and nine days in the mountains. Then they did it all again.

Odin threw in a bonus gift for Skadi. He presented her with two shiny balls. "These are your father's eyes." He tossed them high into the sky, where they transformed into sparkling stars. "Now your father will always be with you. You can look up to find him in the night sky, and he can look down upon you."

SOME PEOPLE BELIEVE THIAZI'S EYES ARE THE BRIGHT TWIN STARS CASTOR AND POLLUX SEEN IN THE GEMINI CONSTELLATION.

THOR'S LOST HAMMER
(OR HOW THOR ALMOST MARRIED A GIANT)

"Where is my hammer?" roared Thor. He rolled out of bed and frantically searched Bilskirnir, his huge hall.

His magic hammer, called Mjollnir, had been made for him by the dwarves. It was the most powerful weapon in Asgard. It always hit its target and always returned to Thor's hand. It kept the gods safe from giants and trolls. Thor never went anywhere without his hammer. He even slept with it. So where was it now?

"Loki!" Thor hurried to find the god of mischief. "Loki! Give me back my hammer!"

Loki swung open his front door. "I don't have your hammer."

Thor waited to hear a story. Loki always tried to talk his way out of trouble when he was guilty. But this time, Loki stayed silent. Thor realized that Loki had not taken his hammer.

"If it wasn't you, that means—" started Thor.

"Your hammer was stolen by a frost giant," finished Loki. "I'll help you find the giant who did it."

"Why would you help me?" Thor asked suspiciously.

"Don't flatter yourself, Thor," said Loki. "I'm not helping you. I'm helping me. Without your hammer, none of us in Asgard are safe."

Loki went to see Freya, the goddess of love and beauty. Freya

sat in a golden chair in her sparkly hall. Two gray cats curled by her feet, waiting eagerly to pull her chariot. She scratched their ears, and they purred. She raised her emerald-green eyes, as Loki entered.

"You look radiant, dear Freya," said Loki. "Truly gorgeous."

Freya ignored Loki's flattery. She knew he couldn't be trusted. "What do you want, Loki?"

"Your falcon cloak," said Loki. "I need it to fly. I'll bring it back when I'm done."

Freya laughed. "Never. I won't lend it out."

"Thor's hammer has been stolen," said Loki.

"Oh, no!" cried Freya. "You must get it back. Take the cloak."

Loki wrapped himself in Freya's cloak of gleaming falcon feathers. With the magic cloak around his shoulders, he soared into the air. He flew swiftly across the nine worlds until he reached Jotunheim, land of the giants. From the sky, he scanned the ground below.

He spotted an ugly giant named Thrym sitting on a rock. Thrym had a bulbous nose, bulging eyes, and tufts of hair growing from his ears. Something about him seemed suspicious.

"Thrym. Good to see you again. Well, no, not really." Loki had been born a giant, but he tried hard to forget that. Visits back here made his skin crawl.

"What do you want?" Thrym grinned mischievously, as if he knew a secret.

"I want what you have," said Loki. "Thor's hammer."

"Leave it to you, sneaky Loki, to figure it out." Thrym gave a deep chuckle. "Yes, I stole Thor's precious hammer. I buried it eight miles under the earth. You'll never get it back, unless . . ."

Loki sighed. "Unless what?"

"Unless I get to marry beautiful Freya," said Thrym.

"How about buckets of gold instead?" offered Loki. "Mountains of gold, in fact."

"I don't want your gold. All I want is Freya. Bring her here, and after our wedding, I will give you back the hammer. Deal?"

Loki didn't answer. He flew back to Asgard and delivered the news.

"Again? Are you out of your mind?" cried Freya. "There's no way I'm marrying that disgusting giant."

"Oh, come on, Freya," said Loki. "I mean—"

"Don't you even start," warned Freya. Her two cats hissed at him. "It will never, ever happen. Get out!"

Odin called the gods and goddesses together. They all agreed that Freya should not be made to marry a giant.

"Then how will I get my hammer back?" demanded Thor.

Odin asked for ideas. But no idea was good. Finally, Heimdall, watchman of the gods, raised his hand. "I may have something."

"Speak," said Odin.

"Thrym wants Freya, so I say we give him Freya. Not the real Freya, but Thor dressed up as Freya," explained Heimdall.

"What?" Thor's face blazed red. "I cannot dress like Freya!"

"Oh, yes, you can," said Odin. "Dressed as a bride, you can sneak into the land of the giants without them knowing who you are. Do it quickly before they attack Asgard. This plan is our best hope to get your hammer back."

"I won't be able to pull it off. I'm not good at things like that," protested Thor.

"I am," Loki told Thor. "I will dress as your maidservant and be by your side. We will trick Thrym together."

The goddesses took Thor and Loki with them. They sewed a long skirt to cover Thor's hairy legs and a blouse that reached across his broad shoulders. They hung Freya's sparkling necklace of the Brislings around his thick neck. Then they covered his face and beard with a wedding veil.

"No one will believe this," grumbled Thor.

"Oh, yes, they will." Loki twirled in his long dress and head scarf. "I look quite beautiful, don't I?"

Thor groaned. He and Loki climbed into his chariot pulled by his two goats, Toothgnasher and Toothgrinder, and set off through the sky to Jotunheim.

The women all took dainty bites and ate small portions. Not Thor. Lifting his veil slightly, he shoveled the food into his mouth, chewing loudly. He ate several whole fish and half the ox on his own. Then he gulped down five large glasses of mead and let out a loud, smelly burp.

"Oh, my!" exclaimed Thrym. "I've never known a goddess with such a big appetite. Are you okay, Freya?"

"She's fine," Loki jumped in. "She was so excited to marry you that she hasn't eaten in days. She's just hungry."

Loki shot Thor a warning look to cool it with the food, but Thor was too busy slurping down cold herring fish to catch it.

"Is it time for the wedding?" Thrym pushed away his own plate.

"Not yet." Loki pointed to the sticky cakes being served. "Can't miss dessert! Best part."

"Let me see my bride's beautiful face." Thrym reached over and tugged Thor's veil before Loki could stop him. Thrym gasped. "Freya's eyes glow red like fire. Why is she so angry?"

"It's not fire. It's the fire of happiness," said Loki quickly. "She's so happy that she has not slept."

"As it should be." Thrym grinned. "It's time for us to get married. Bring me Thor's hammer," he told his servant.

They landed close to the rock where Thrym still sat.

"Keep your face down and let me do the talking," Loki whispered to Thor. "Thrym, my friend. We have traveled for eight days and eight nights, and I have brought your bride-to-be."

Thrym lumbered to his gnarly feet and clapped his swollen hands in delight. "Freya is here! We will have a wedding tonight."

He instructed his servants to prepare a wedding feast.

That night, Thor and Loki—dressed as Freya and her maid—joined Thrym and his guests at his long table. Thrym insisted the bride sit at his right side. Loki, the maid, sat to his left.

Plates of roasted meats with savory sauces were piled on the table, along with a whole ox and several of the largest fish Thor had ever seen. He licked his lips under the veil. Thor was hungry, and the food smelled delicious.

Thor let out a cry when he saw his mighty hammer, but Loki talked over him. "The hammer must rest in the bride's lap as you say your vows. It's for good luck. That's how it is done in Asgard."

Thrym agreed, and the servant placed the hammer on Thor's lap. Thor wrapped his hand around the familiar handle. Then he let out a thunderous roar and stood to his full height. Pushing back his veil, he threw the hammer at Thrym.

It hit the giant squarely between the eyes, killing him instantly. Then the trusty hammer returned to Thor's hand.

"Let's crush more giants!" cried Thor.

"Let's just get out of here." Loki pulled Thor toward the chariot, both of them tripping over their long skirts as the giants chased them.

They flew back to Asgard, bringing Thor's hammer with them.

Thor never lost it again.

Frey and Gerd
(or A Sword for Love)

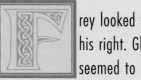rey looked to his left. He looked to his right. Gladsheim, Odin's great hall, seemed to be empty. No gods or servants were about. Odin was traveling in Midgard disguised as an old man. Frey, god of the harvest, gazed up at Odin's golden throne. *Did he dare?*

Only Odin was allowed to sit on his high throne.

From here, Odin could view all of the nine worlds. Sometimes Frigg, goddess of love and beauty, sat there, but that was an entirely other thing. She was his wife, after all.

Frey couldn't control his curiosity. *A quick look*, he reasoned. *That won't be so bad.*

He sat on the throne. His eyes widened in amazement. He could see everything! He saw a ladybug on a leaf in Alfheim, land of the Light Elves. He saw an earthworm wriggling underground in Nidavellir, land of the dwarves. And in Jotunheim, land of the giants, he saw . . .

Frey sucked in his breath. He saw the most beautiful giantess ever. Her blond hair hung in two long braids, and her snow-white skin glowed in the sunlight. Frey's heart squeezed in his chest. Frey wandered back home to Alfheim, thinking only of the beauty he'd just seen. He couldn't eat or sleep. All he could do was dream of her. Who was she?

Frey soon learned that she was Gerd, daughter of the giant Gymir. She was known far and

wide for the brilliant light that shined around her. There was no way she would ever love him back.

For days, Frey refused to come out of his room. He feared his unhappiness was punishment for sitting on the throne. He stopped sending sunlight into the world. He stopped making rain. Crops turned brown and died.

Frey's father, Njord, god of the seas, grew concerned. He sent for Skirnir, Frey's trusty Light Elf messenger. "My son talks to you. Find out what troubles him. Please, do whatever it takes to make Frey happy again."

"I'm in love with Gerd," Frey confessed to Skirnir. "A god can't ask a giantess to marry him, so I will remain forever sad without her. And even if I could go to her, she'd never agree to be with me. She glows with incredible beauty."

"What if I go to her for you?" asked Skirnir.

"Would you really?" Frey grabbed Skirnir's shoulders. "It's a long, dangerous journey."

"I'll go if you give me your horse. Your horse can leap through fire," said Skirnir. "And your sword, too."

Frey's sword had been a gift from the dwarves. It could fight giants and trolls by itself. It didn't need a hand to hold it. The sword was his most

prized treasure, but his love for Gerd was greater.

"Both treasures are yours if you can convince Gerd to marry me," said Frey.

Skirnir rode off on Frey's horse with Frey's gleaming sword in his hand. Magic flames burned around Gymir's hall in Jotunheim, but Frey's horse jumped through them. Skirnir pushed past the barking guard dogs and entered the giant's hall. Luckily, the giant wasn't at home.

"I've been sent by my master, the god Frey," he told Gerd. "He would very much like to marry you." Skirnir told stories about how great Frey was. How smart and

generous. How people in Midgard loved him. Skirnir reached into the sack he carried. "I brought eleven golden apples of youth from Idunn's tree for you—"

"I don't want apples." Gerd waved Skirnir away. "I mean, I should hope I'm worth more than a bunch of magic apples. Besides, I don't want to marry Frey."

"I have something better." Skirnir pulled a gold armband from his sack. "This is made from the thickest gold."

"Stop trying to buy me," said Gerd. "I don't want gold, and I don't want Frey to be my husband."

Skirnir was getting desperate. He drew his sword. "If you don't marry Frey, I will cut off your head."

Gerd laughed a big belly laugh. She wasn't scared. "If you touch one hair on my head, my father will come for you. Trust me. You do not want that."

Gerd put away the sword and reached into his sack once more. He pulled out a magic wand. He cast a spell on Gerd. "If you refuse to marry Frey, you will turn uglier than the ugliest troll. You will grow old. Your skin will wrinkle, and your bones will ache."

Gerd didn't want to turn ugly and old. "You win. Reverse your spell.

I'll marry your god." She agreed to meet Frey in the forest in nine nights to be married.

Skirnir returned to Alfheim and told Frey the happy news.

"Nine nights?" Frey didn't think he could wait that long. His heart overflowed with so much love.

For nine nights, Gerd worried if she'd made a mistake. Was keeping her beauty worth it?

But Gerd showed up in the forest as she'd promised. "I'm here," she said to Frey unhappily.

Frey got down on one knee. He told Gerd how much he cared for her and respected her. He apologized for his servant's harsh ways. He didn't want her to do anything she didn't want to.

Frey wrapped her in a hug. Much to Gerd's surprise, her heart began to glow even brighter. She hugged him back. She knew then that he'd always be good to her, and they'd be happy together.

At that moment, the sun shone, rain fell, and flowers bloomed again.

Frey smiled, but up in Asgard, Odin frowned. He knew Ragnarok was coming, and when it did, Frey would wish he hadn't traded away his magic sword for love.

Thor Looks for Adventure
(or The Giant King)

hor twirled his hammer. All was quiet in Asgard. The wall stood strong. No giants or trolls tried to come in. The gods played games and relaxed.

"I'm bored," the god of thunder told Loki.

"You can't wait for fun to find you. You have to make your own fun," said Loki. "What do you like to do?"

Thor didn't need to think. "Fight giants."

"Road trip to Jotunheim!" cried Loki.

"You and me?" Thor was surprised.

"I'm up for an adventure," said Loki.

More like up for trouble, thought Thor.

Thor and Loki set off in Thor's bronze chariot pulled by Thor's two prized goats, Toothgrinder and Toothgnasher. By sunset, they'd reached the border where Midgard met Jotunheim.

Thor pointed to a small farmhouse. "Let's stop here for the night."

They unhitched the goats and knocked on the door. The farmer who answered almost toppled over in shock when he saw two gods looming before him. He quickly invited them in.

The house was simple and tidy. The farmer showed them straw mats where they could sleep. The farmer's wife took out a small loaf of brown bread. "This is all the food we have."

Thor looked at the farmer, his wife, and their skinny daughter and son. "Thank you, but we brought our own food."

"We did?" Loki hadn't remembered packing anything.

"We did." Thor went outside and slaughtered Toothgrinder and Toothgnasher. He skinned them and roasted them over a fire.

"Eat as much as you'd like," Thor told the family. "All I ask is that you don't crack any bones, and you return all the bones here." He pointed to the goatskins that he'd spread beside the fire. "I will need them later."

Thor ate one whole goat himself. He gave the other to Loki and the family.

The family feasted. Thialfi, the farmer's son, ate until his stomach was painfully full.

Loki pulled the boy aside and whispered mischievously into his ear, "You want to know a secret? The marrow inside the bones is the best part. Delicious! It's the food of the gods."

So when no one was looking, young Thialfi cracked a thighbone in half and sucked out the juicy marrow. It was good! Then he buried the cracked bone under the pile of bones on the goatskin.

At the first light of dawn the next morning, Thor went outside and stood before the pile of bones. He wrapped them in the goatskins and waved Mjollnir, his magic hammer. Poof! Toothgrinder and Toothgnasher sprang back to life, as if they hadn't just been eaten for dinner.

Toothgrinder pranced about, but Toothgnasher gave a cry. He was limping. The goat's leg was broken.

Thor let out a thundering roar that woke the entire family.

"Who did this?" His thick hand tightened around his hammer's handle, and his biceps bulged. "I asked for only one thing! Someone disobeyed. I will turn your house into rubble!"

The farmer, his wife, and their daughter shook with fear. "Please don't hurt us."

Thialfi understood the danger he'd put his family in. "It was me. I didn't mean to hurt your goat. I'm really sorry. Please don't punish my family. I will do anything to repay you. I will be your servant."

Thor snorted. "Why would I want a puny boy like you for my servant?"

"I can run really fast," said Thialfi. "I'm the fastest in these lands."

"That's true," said Thialfi's sister, Roskva. "I'll be your servant, too. We can both run errands for you."

"I vote we take the skinny boy with us," Loki said, tweaking the boy's ear. "No need to punish the whole family."

By this time, Thor's anger had disappeared. He agreed. He put Roskva in charge of his two goats. "Keep them safe until I return. We're off to fight giants."

Thor, Loki, and Thialfi traveled east. The land was rocky and wild. The cold wind pushed against them as they cut paths through the thick underbrush. Exhausted, they sent Thialfi to search for a place to sleep as the sun set.

Thialfi couldn't find anything, and he moved deeper into the forest. Then he saw the strangest house.

It looked almost like a cave with a big opening but no door or windows. He brought Thor and Loki inside. Five long halls branched off a large main room. They made a fire in the main room and fell asleep.

In the middle of the night, the ground shook violently and jolted them awake.

"W-w-what was that?" cried Thialfi.

"Earthquake," said Loki. "Big one."

The land continued to rumble and shake. Loki and Thialfi moved into a side hall. Thor stayed in the main room, alert and on watch.

In the morning, Thor stepped outside. He rubbed his eyes, bleary from not sleeping, and tried to make sense of what he found.

The biggest, most massive giant lay fast asleep on his back. With huge, gasping breaths, the giant let out earth-shaking snores. This was the earthquake they had felt all night. The giant was bigger than a mountain! Thor touched Megingjord, his magical belt, to double his strength. At that moment, the giant opened his enormous eyes. He yawned, letting out a blast of hot air.

"Hello?" Thor wasn't afraid.

"Hello there, little one," the giant boomed. "I'm Skrymir. That means 'big fellow' in giant language. My mother had a sense of humor, because I'm the smallest in our family." He looked at his huge hands. One wore a leather glove. The other was bare. "Where's my glove? Have you seen it?"

Thor shook his head.

"Ah, there it is!" The giant reached over and grabbed his glove. As he did, Loki and Thialfi tumbled out. The cave they'd spent the night in was really a giant's glove!

"Going into Jotunheim?" asked Skrymir. "Okay if we go together?"

Thor looked at Loki. Loki shrugged. "Sure."

"Breakfast first," said the giant. He ate four oxen, six goats, and a dozen fish. Thor, Loki, and Thialfi shared some fruit and the bread from the farmer's wife.

"Give me your pack of food," said Skrymir. "I will carry it on our journey. You will need all your energy to keep up with me."

They handed over their sack and set off into the wilderness. Each step the giant took covered miles of land. Thor, Loki, and Thialfi tried to keep his head in sight through the clouds as they climbed mountains and pushed through pine forests.

By nightfall, they finally caught up to Skrymir, who was snoozing in a valley. "I already ate. Your food is in my sack." He closed his eyes and began to snore. The ground rumbled.

Loki climbed up the sack and tried to untie it. The laces wouldn't budge. It was magically sealed tight. "We've been tricked!"

Thor was hungry, and he grew angry. He would teach this giant a lesson. He stepped onto Skrymir's forehead and stood between his eyebrows. Then he brought his hammer down hard into Skrymir's skull.

Skrymir opened one eye. "Did a leaf land on my head?"

He closed his eye and fell back asleep.

Now Thor was super angry. He climbed back onto the snoring giant. He pounded the giant's head with his hammer once more.

The giant's eyes fluttered open. "I think an acorn just fell on my head. Thor? What are you doing up there? You should get some shut-eye." And he went back to sleep.

Thor was still awake when the sun rose. He'd spent the night fuming and thinking about how hungry he was.

"Good morning!" Skrymir's booming voice woke Loki and Thialfi. "Listen, folks, it's been fun, but we need to part ways. I'm going north. You're heading east toward Utgard. I must warn you—the giants there make me look small. I suggest you go someplace else. Safety first, I always say."

The giant stomped away, each footstep causing an earthquake.

"We're going to Utgard," growled Thor. "I'm hungry and the fortress of the giants will have food."

By midday, they reached Utgard. The fortress walls, carved from ice blocks, were so high they had to crane their necks to see the tops. Noise and merriment came from inside.

They called out, but no one answered.

"I vote we let ourselves in." Loki pointed to the huge metal gate. The bars were spaced to keep out giants, but the three of them easily slipped through.

Thor walked bravely forward, and Loki and Thialfi followed. They entered a massive hall, where giants feasted and laughed. The giant king sat on a huge throne.

"What do we have here? Small visitors!" the king boomed. "You must be Thor, god of thunder.

Your reputation is much bigger than you are, that's for sure." He laughed heartily at his own joke. "I hope you're stronger than you look."

Thor clutched his hammer. He did not like this rude giant king one bit.

"And you must be Loki. I am Utgard-Loki. We share the same name. Maybe it means we're related, do you think?" boomed the giant.

"I doubt it." Loki was irritated, too.

"So tell me, what are you little people good at? I only let those with amazing skills share my food," said Utgard-Loki. "What's your thing, Loki?"

"I can eat really fast," said Loki.

"You don't say. Let's put you to the test." Utgard-Loki called over a giant named Logi. He had a servant set down a trough filled with roasted meat. There were oxen, rabbits, deer, and goats. Loki sat at one end. Logi sat at the other end.

"Ready, set, eat!" cried Utgard-Loki.

Loki shoveled the meat into his mouth. So did Logi. They both chewed and swallowed at lightning speed. They met in the middle of the trough at the same time. Loki had eaten all his meat. Logi had eaten all his meat—and he had eaten all the bones and even the wooden trough itself!

"Logi is the winner," declared the giant king.

Loki scowled. Utgard-Loki turned his gaze on Thialfi. "You, small boy. What can you do?"

"I can run," said Thialfi.

Utgard-Loki laughed. "We will have a running race."

They went outside. Utgard-Loki called over a small giant named Hugi. "See how fair I am, servant boy? I won't make you run against a full-size giant. That post over there is the finish line. Go!"

Thialfi ran faster than a rabbit chased by a fox, faster than a sailfish in the ocean, and faster that a cheetah in the wild. But Hugi easily beat him to the finish line.

"Your boy is fast, but not fast enough," Utgard-Loki said to Thor. "Now you."

"I can drink more than anyone," boasted Thor.

They went back inside the great hall. Utgard-Loki had his drinking horn brought forward. "Many giants can finish this in one drink. Some take two. Everyone in my kingdom can finish it in three. Let's see what you can do."

The drinking horn was longer than any drinking horn Thor had ever seen. He raised the horn to his lips. Mead flowed down his throat. Thor gulped and gulped until, at last, he was sure he'd drained it all. He put down the horn and peered inside.

The horn was still filled with mead!

Utgard-Loki shook his head in disappointment. "Maybe you can do it with a second drink."

Thor raised it to his lips once more. He took long swallows, drinking and drinking. Yet when he stopped, the mead had only gone down an inch.

Thor tried for a third time. Still, the mead barely went down.

"This is nonsense!" cried Thor.

"Very well. Let's try something else. Can you pick up a cat?" asked Utgard-Loki.

"Are you serious? Of course," said Thor.

Utgard-Loki pointed to a large gray cat sleeping on the floor. "Pick her up."

Thor bent his knees and slid his arms under the cat's furry belly. He strained and struggled. The cat would not budge. He wrapped his arms around the cat and tried to yank her up. The cat still did not move.

"Children can lift a cat, Thor," shouted Utgard-Loki. Laughter echoed throughout the hall.

Fury gathered inside Thor. He used every bit of strength and pulled. The cat arched its back. As Thor stretched, the cat arched higher and higher, but her paws never left the ground.

"Forget it, Thor. You're upsetting my cat," said Utgard-Loki. "Face facts. You're not strong."

Thor looked around at all the towering giants. "I will wrestle any one of you!"

"Wrestle? Well, okay. I will choose your opponent." Utgard-Loki smirked. "Elle, come here." A shriveled woman with steel-gray hair hobbled forward leaning on a walking stick. "This is Elle, my old nurse. She shall wrestle you."

Thor stepped back. "No, I couldn't. . . she's old. . . ."

Before Thor could finish, Elle dropped her cane and grabbed Thor in a choke hold. Thor wrestled back, bending and turning. She twisted his arm, and he twisted hers. She kicked his feet out from under him. Thor fell to one knee but refused to go all the way to the ground.

"I used illusion, a type of magic, to make myself appear so large. And when you kept hitting my head with your hammer while I was pretending to sleep, it wasn't my head you were hitting. I used illusion to replace my head with those mountains over there."

He pointed to two mountains that now had chunks chipped out of their middles. "Otherwise, you would've really hurt me."

"What about all those contests?" asked Loki.

"The giant Logi, who won the eating contest, wasn't a real giant. He was wildfire. No one can consume more than a burning wildfire," explained Utgard-Loki. "Thialfi wasn't racing against a giant. He was racing against Thought. There's no outrunning your thoughts."

"What about the drinking horn?" demanded Thor.

"The other end was dipped into the ocean, which never runs dry. You drank so much that your created tides. From now on, because of you, the sea level will rise and fall," said Utgard-Loki. "The cat was really Jormungand, the serpent who wraps itself around Midgard. The Midgard serpent is impossible to lift, yet you almost did."

"And your old nurse?" asked Thor.

"Elle wasn't a woman, but Old Age. Old Age weakens us, then defeats us in the end. Yet you wouldn't fall, Thor." Utgard-Loki crossed his arms. "Now that I have seen your powers, I will use my magic to make sure you never come here again."

"Oh yeah?" Thor raised his hammer to pound this deceiving giant.

"Done!" Utgard-Loki clapped.

Thor hobbled away with his head hung in shame.

"Excellent games! Now let's eat. Join us, Thor, Loki, and Thialfi," said Utgard-Loki.

Loki and Thialfi poked at their food. Thor ate heartily, but he was angry and embarrassed. *Will the giant king let everyone in the nine worlds know how weak I've become?* he wondered.

After the meal, the three headed for the fortress door. Utgard-Loki followed. "Hold on. I tricked you."

Loki raised his eyebrows. "You tricked us?"

"Yes. I was Skrymir, the giant you met the other night. I'd heard you were journeying to Utgard, and I was worried. I came to meet you."

"I don't understand," said Thor.

Then he blinked.

Utgard-Loki had vanished. The fortress had vanished, too.

They stood by themselves in a field of snow.

"Bravo!" cried Loki. "What excellent trickery."

"What do we do now?" asked Thialfi.

"We go home," said Loki. "We've had enough adventure for today, haven't we, Thor?"

Thor nodded. But he wasn't done with adventure, not quite yet. He needed to find a way to destroy the Midgard serpent. But first he'd go back to the farm.

His two goats were waiting for him.

The Dreams of Balder
(or Watch Out for the Mistletoe)

alder, the god of light, was the kindest god in all of Asgard. He always had something nice to say. He'd help anyone with anything. He was sweet and patient with his blind brother, Hod. Goodness glowed from within Balder and made him beautiful.

All the gods loved Balder. All except Loki.

Loki complained that Balder was too nice, too good, and too handsome. In truth, Loki was jealous. Balder was everything the mischief maker wasn't. Even when he tried to be good, evil and trouble had a way of finding Loki.

Balder was married to Nanna, who loved him greatly. When Balder began having bad dreams, Nanna grew worried. In his dreams, he saw a flash of red and then darkness. He saw Hel, queen of the underworld, getting ready to welcome him. In every dream, he died.

His mother, Frigg, and his father, Odin, were shocked to see their son so sad and scared. Frigg hugged Balder tightly, then turned to Odin. "Go to Hel and find out what's going on!"

Odin, the All-Father, hated traveling down into the darkness of Niflheim. But he knew better than to argue with his wife, especially when she was upset about their son.

Odin mounted his eight-legged horse, Sleipnir, and galloped over the rainbow bridge out of Asgard. Sleipnir was the fastest horse in all the worlds. They rode for days, until rugged land gave way to swirling mist and heavy dark clouds. The air turned bitter cold, and all light disappeared. They had entered the land of the dead. Sleipnir cantered in total darkness, her hooves crunching the icy snow. They finally reached a tall iron gate.

Odin banged on it with his spear. "Hel! I've come to speak with you!"

Hel, daughter of Loki, appeared in a swirl of frosty air. The rotting skin covering half her face hung off the bone. Hel was half beautiful girl and half rotting corpse.

"You've come to visit?" Hel was surprised. She never had visitors. "You picked a busy day."

Behind her, dead servants were preparing a welcome feast.

"Who's this all for?" Odin dreaded the answer.

"Balder," Hel said coldly.

Odin returned to Asgard. He told Frigg the sad news. Balder would soon die.

"No!" wailed Frigg. "I won't let my brilliant son go to Hel."

Odin shook his head. "It's his fate. The three Norns, who sit by the roots of Yggdrasil, decide what's to be, and there's nothing you or I can do."

"Nonsense! I'm his mother. I'll make sure my boy lives." When Frigg set her mind to something, nothing could stop her.

Frigg traveled throughout all nine worlds. She made everyone and everything promise not to harm Balder. Every god, giant, troll, dwarf, and elf promised. Every animal promised—from the biggest blue whale to the smallest ant. All the trees and plants—from the towering oak to the lowly dandelion—promised. Water promised not to drown him. Fire promised not to burn him. Serpents promised not to poison him. Stones and iron promised not to bruise him. Arrows and spears promised not to pierce him. Rain, snow, wind, and fog promised not to get him lost or sick. The sun promised not to burn him.

Everything in all the worlds took the oath. Frigg told Balder he would now be safe.

"Let's see if it really works." Loki threw an apple. It bounced off Balder's forehead.

Balder grinned. "Didn't hurt a bit."

Other gods gathered around Balder, who stood by the Well of Urd, and made a game of it. They threw plates and jugs. They threw stones and spears. They shot arrows. Nothing harmed Balder. The gods cheered.

Loki hated seeing Balder celebrated. But how could he put an end to a god who could never be hurt?

That afternoon, an old woman dressed in black shuffled into Frigg's hall. The queen of the Aesir offered the stranger a seat at her table. The old woman listened as Frigg told the other goddesses about how she'd saved Balder.

The old woman whispered into Frigg's ear, "Did you really get everything to take an oath?"

"Of course," said Frigg.

"You didn't miss anything?" asked the old woman. "Come on, you can tell me."

"I do," said Hod. "But since I'm blind, I can't see where to throw anything."

"I'll help you aim your arrow."

Loki sneakily attached a piece of mistletoe to the tip of an arrow. He watched Hod thread the arrow into his bow. Loki guided Hod's hand so the arrow lined up with Balder's heart.

"Now," said Loki.

Just as Hod shot the arrow, Balder raised his head and saw a flash of red. It was the same flash of red he'd seen in his dreams. But it was too late. The arrow pierced his body. Darkness surrounded him, and he dropped to the ground and died.

Frigg's and Nanna's cries echoed throughout the nine worlds. Birds stopped singing. The sun dimmed. Petals wilted. Hod wept when he realized his beautiful brother had died because of him.

The gods grabbed Hod, but then spotted Loki. They knew the mischief maker had somehow helped cause Balder's death. But before they could do anything, Loki ran away as fast as he could.

Tears streamed down Frigg's face as she covered Balder's body with a white sheet. "Someone must go

"Well . . . I did skip over one small piece of mistletoe," admitted Frigg. "The creeping vine lives on a tree to the west of Valhalla. It's young and can't survive on its own. Surely it's nothing to worry about."

Suddenly, the old woman yawned. "It's way past my bedtime." She left the hall and disappeared. A while later (after a quick stop to a tree west of Valhalla), Loki returned to the Well of Urd. He stood beside Balder's twin brother, Hod. They listened to the gods laugh as they threw vegetables and stones at Balder.

"You look sad," he said to Hod. "I bet you want to join the fun."

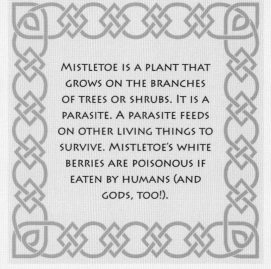

MISTLETOE IS A PLANT THAT GROWS ON THE BRANCHES OF TREES OR SHRUBS. IT IS A PARASITE. A PARASITE FEEDS ON OTHER LIVING THINGS TO SURVIVE. MISTLETOE'S WHITE BERRIES ARE POISONOUS IF EATEN BY HUMANS (AND GODS, TOO!).

to Hel and bring my boy's soul back. Perhaps she will listen to reason or accept a ransom to return Balder to us. But it can't be you, Odin. She doesn't like you."

Hermod stepped forward. "I will do it, Mother."

Hermod, the messenger god, was also Frigg and Odin's son.

"Are you sure?" asked Odin. "Few who visit Hel return."

Hermod nodded bravely. Odin lent him Sleipnir, for the eight-legged horse knew the way to Hel. Hermod and Sleipnir galloped off at top speed. It would take them nine days to reach the eternal darkness.

Meanwhile, the gods wrapped Balder's body and placed him gently on a special longboat. They would send him out to sea for his funeral. His wife, Nanna, was so upset that she died of a broken heart. The gods placed her body next to Balder's.

During this time, Odin had another son with the giantess Rind. His name was Váli. When Váli was just one day old (he'd grown into a man super quickly), he killed Hod for killing Balder.

Hermod, on the back of Sleipnir, finally crossed the bridge that led into the icy mist and gloom of Niflheim. The stallion leaped over Hel's enormous iron gate.

Hermod entered the great hall of the dead. Balder and Nanna sat with other souls at a long table. Light no longer shone from Balder. His skin looked gray and his eyes were dull. Hermod walked toward the tall throne at the back of the hall.

"The brother has arrived," sneered Hel when she spotted Hermod.

"Balder is so greatly missed throughout the world," said Hermod. "Please, let me bring him back."

Hel tapped her long fingernails together. "Let's do a test. Ask every god, every giant, every dwarf, every animal, every plant, every stone, every . . . well, you get the idea, if they will cry for Balder. If everything weeps, he will be returned to the land of the living. If just one thing refuses, he will be forever mine."

"I will not," she said. "Balder thought he was so great. Well, he wasn't. Hel can keep him."

Hermod gasped. Now Balder was doomed to stay in the land of the dead. Hermod returned to Asgard with the news.

Frigg cried for a long time then wiped away her tears. "Only one giantess, you say? And you didn't recognize her?" Frigg's eyes now flashed with fury. "That must have been Loki in disguise."

"Loki caused all of this," said Odin.

"I'm going to find him." Thor grabbed his mighty hammer. "This time he'll be sorry when I do."

Hermod and Sleipnir journeyed out of the darkness. For months, he traveled to every corner of each of the nine worlds and asked everyone and everything he met if they'd weep for Balder.

Fire wept. Clouds wept. Butterflies wept. Dark elves wept. Squid wept. Gods wept. Giants wept. Rivers wept. Dragons wept. Everything wept.

Hermod had done it! Soon Balder would be going home. But just as he was ready to leave Jotunheim, Hermod stumbled across an old giantess he'd never seen before.

"Will you weep for Balder?" Hermod waited for her to agree.

Punishment for Loki
(or How Loki Was Caught by His Own Net)

sgard wasn't the same without Balder. Clouds filled the once-cloudless skies. Glittery roofs didn't shine. Gods no longer hummed merry tunes. Frigg cried for her son, and Odin feared the end was near.

The sea gods, Aegir and Ran, decided to throw a feast to cheer up the gods. Thor was still gone, searching for Loki, but everyone else came. Delicious food was served at long tables. For the first time in a long time, the gods began to smile.

Then Loki walked in. The gods stared.

Loki drank a horn of mead from a large cauldron. He ate roasted meat. He ate and drank some more.

The gods stayed far away from the mischief maker. No one wanted to ruin the party. But Loki hated being ignored. He needed to be the center of attention.

So he began to speak. He made fun of Idunn's apples, teased Bragi about his poetry, and insulted Sif's hair. He mocked Njord's pretty feet and hissed at Freya's cats.

"Enough!" boomed Odin. "Loki, you are not welcome here."

Loki laughed. "You cannot kick me out, Odin. We're brothers. You took an oath to always have my back."

"True." Odin sighed. "But your evil cannot continue. If I cannot stop you, then—"

"I will!" Thor burst through the wooden doors of the hall. His huge body blocked all light from outside. He raised his hammer. "Mjollnir will help me."

"No need for the hammer. I was just leaving. This party's lame." Loki darted around Thor and raced away.

He ran as fast as he could to a cabin he'd built on top of a mountain by the sea. The cabin had four open doors, so he could see danger approaching from the north, south, east, and west.

Loki knew Thor would hunt for him and punish him. And he knew Odin wouldn't stop him this time.

He needed a clever place to hide—and a good disguise.

Loki changed into a salmon. He swam in a pool at the bottom of a waterfall during the day. At night, he sat by the fire in his house.

What if Thor finds the waterfall? What if he discovers the salmon is really me? Could he catch me? Loki wondered. *Not with his bare hands, for I'd dart away. And not with a hook. But if he had something else . . .*

Loki schemed. He twisted rope and began to tie knots. He braided the very first fishing net.

Suddenly, he heard a noise. He looked out his door facing west. The gods were climbing the mountain, and Thor was leading the pack. Odin had spotted Loki's cabin from his high throne. They were coming for him.

Loki flung the net into the fire. He dove into the waterfall and changed into a salmon, just as the gods burst into the cabin.

"Loki's gone!" roared Thor.

"Look at this." Njord, god of the seas, pulled the ashes of the net from the fire with a stick.

Thor scratched his beard. "Look at what?"

"It's a net to catch fish," Njord marveled. "Loki's quite clever."

"I can make one." Tyr found a ball of rope on the floor. He tied knots, following the crisscross pattern of the ashes.

"Take it with us," said Njord. "Let's go!"

"Take what? Go where?" Thor wished they would stop playing guessing games.

"To the pool at the bottom of that waterfall," said Njord. "This net will help us catch fish. I bet Loki is one of them."

SALMON ARE ONE OF A FEW FISH THAT SWIM UPSTREAM. VIKINGS BELIEVED THAT WHEN THOR GRABBED LOKI THE SALMON, HE CAUSED THE FISH TO HAVE A TAPERED TAIL.

"I totally knew that." Thor held one end of the net. The other gods held the other end. They dragged it across the pool.

Loki's salmon heart beat fast. He wouldn't be able to swim downstream and out to sea without being tangled in the net. He had only one choice for escape. Loki the Salmon swam up the waterfall!

The gods were amazed. They'd never seen a fish swim upstream before.

"It's Loki!" cried Thor. The gods raced to the top of the waterfall with the net.

As Loki the Salmon tried to jump over the waterfall, Thor reached out his mighty hand and grabbed him by his tail. Loki struggled, but Thor squeezed his tail tightly.

The salmon changed back into Loki form. The gods dragged him into a deep cave and tied him to three flat rocks. Skadi, daughter of the dead giant Thiazi, entered the cave. She hung a poisonous snake above Loki's head. The gods wanted him to suffer for Balder's death, but they didn't want to kill him. They allowed Loki's wife, Sigyn, to sit by his side.

Sigyn held up a bowl to catch the poison before it dripped into Loki's open mouth. But when the bowl was full, she had to leave to quickly empty it into a bubbling pit. The snake's fangs still dripped poison, and the venom landed in Loki's eyes, burning them. He cried out in pain and shook so violently that the ground in Midgard shook with him. Sigyn hurried to return with her bowl, and the cycle went on and on and on. . . .

Loki, Sigyn, and the snake will stay trapped in the cave . . . until Ragnarok comes.

Ragnarok
(or How It All Ends)

We have finished with stories from the past, so now it's time to look to the future. It is a future that Odin can see with his one eye long before it will happen. The All-Father trembles, because he broke his oath and allowed the gods to hurt his oath-brother, Loki. He shivers, because in the future, winter will not end. The cold, whipping winds will blow more frigid than ever before. The stars will disappear. Darkness will fall.

Humans in Midgard will fight—not only their enemies but also their friends and families. Wars will rage. Forests will burn. Mountains will crack. Gods will fight, too. The Valkyries will gather as many fallen

heroes as they can, but Valhalla will soon grow too full. The dragon Nidhogg will chew through the thick roots of Yggdrasil. The World Tree will tilt and its leaves will turn brown.

Ragnarok will come.

When it does, Loki will escape the poisonous snake and break free. He will call all who are evil to side with him against the gods. Hel will rise up from Niflheim. Fenrir the wolf will tear through the magic ribbon that holds him. Jormungand, the Midgard serpent, will bring the seas crashing over the land.

Loki will command *Naglfar*, a ship made from the fingernails of the dead. His children and the ghosts of the dead from Niflheim will sail with him. Garm, the vicious dog who guards Hel's hall, will break his chains and bound onto the boat. Surt, the fire demon, will leave the fiery world of Muspell to join Loki's army. Frost giants will march in from the east. Together, they will all head to Asgard.

At the Bifrost, Heimdall will spot them long before they approach. The watchman will raise Gjallerhorn and trumpet the call, signaling to the gods that they must grab their weapons. Odin will ride eight-legged Sleipnir to Mimir's Well to ask Mimir's head what to do. Mimir's head will whisper to Odin, and what its words say will give Odin hope for the future.

Odin will call to the dead heroes in Valhalla to join the fight on the side of the gods. They will ride to a great field where Loki and his army awaits. This will be the final battle. This will be Ragnarok.

It will be a battle that goes on for days. Hooves will pound. Swords will clash. Gods will fall. Giants will fall.

Frey will battle Surt, who holds a flaming sword brighter than a thousand suns. Frey's sword will be no match for the fire giant, and he will wish he hadn't given away his magic sword to win Gerd's heart. Frey will be the first god to die.

Odin will raise his spear, Gungnir, and go after Fenrir. The fight will be frightful. Fenrir will open his huge jaws and, with a snap, swallow the All-Father whole.

Thor cannot help Odin, for he will be in battle with the Midgard serpent. Thor's mighty hammer will crash against the serpent's poisonous coils. Mjollnir will crush the serpent dead just as its coils squeeze the air from Thor's lungs and its fangs poison him. Thor will untangle himself and walk nine steps before falling to the ground, dead.

Vidar, Odin's son who has not done much until now, will hurry to avenge Odin's death. Using his immense strength, Vidar will press open the wolf's lower jaw with his boot. His boot is made from scraps of leather left over from all the shoes ever made in the world. Vidar will grab Fenrir's upper jaw and yank it back, ripping the horrible wolf in half.

Garm, Hel's snarling dog, will fight brave Tyr, and they will both die.

Heimdall will stand against Loki. They will pierce and kill each other with their swords.

The fire from Surt's blazing sword will ignite the nine worlds and drown them in flames and smoke. The two wolves will finally catch and swallow the Sun and the Moon. The earth will sink into the sea, and all will be destroyed.

Well, not all.

Before the Sun is swallowed, she will give birth to a daughter. The daughter will bring light and warmth back to the sky. Rivers will flow. Animals will graze. Plants will grow.

Thor's sons, Modi and Magni, will survive Ragnarok. Together, they will be strong enough to hold their father's mighty hammer. Hoenir will come from Vanaheim and help them rule a new generation of gods. Odin's sons Vidar and Váli will also make it through the battle. Balder and Hod will return to the land of the living. In total, seven Aesir will survive.

Yggdrasil will stay alive and sprout new leaves. Two humans will step out from inside its trunk. The World Tree's thick bark will have kept them safe, and its morning dew will have fed them. Their names will be Life and The Will to Live. They will give birth to children, who will populate the earth.

And the world will begin again. And again.

"Life is a circle," wise Mimir said to Odin. "When one journey ends a new one begins. It will never be THE END."

THE NUMBER 9
QUIZ
THE NUMBER 9 APPEARS
MANY TIMES IN THE NORSE
MYTHS. CAN YOU FIND
THEM ALL?
SEE PAGE 95 FOR ANSWERS.

NUMBER 9 QUIZ ANSWERS

THERE ARE 9 WORLDS.

·

ODIN HANGS ON YGGDRASIL FOR 9 DAYS AND NIGHTS.

·

EVERY 9 DAYS, ODIN'S ARM RING, DRAUPNIR, MAKES 8 RINGS, FOR A TOTAL OF 9 RINGS.

·

FREY MUST WAIT 9 NIGHTS TO MARRY GERD.

·

IT TAKES 9 DAYS FOR HERMOD TO TRAVEL TO HEL.

·

AEGIR AND RAN HAVE 9 DAUGHTERS (THE WAVES), WHO ARE ALL HEIMDALL'S MOTHERS.

·

NJORD AND SKADI AGREE TO SPEND 9 NIGHTS BY THE SEA AND 9 NIGHTS IN THE MOUNTAINS.

·

AT RAGNAROK, THOR TAKES 9 STEPS BEFORE FALLING DEAD.

How to Say Norse Names
A Pronunciation Guide

Aegir: *ai-geer*

Aesir: *ai-seer*

Alfheim: *ahlf-hame*

Angrboda: *ahng-ger-boh-duh*

Asgard: *ahs-gahrd*

Ask: *ahs-k*

Audumla: *ow-doom-la*

Balder: *bahl-der*

Bergelmir: *berg-ell-mere*

Bestla: *bes-tla*

Bifrost: *bye-frost*

Bor: *bohr*

Bragi: *brah-gee*

Brokk: *brock*

Buri: *bu-ree*

Draupnir: *drawp-neer*

Eitri: *ay-tree*

Elle: *ell-lee*

Embla: *em-bler*

Fenrir: *fen-reer*

Frey: *fray*

Freya: *fray-ah*

Frigg: *frigg*

Garm: *gahrm*

Gerd: *gaird*

Ginnungagap: *gin-noon-gah-gahp*

Gjallerhorn: *gyat-lar-horn*

Gleipnir: *glayp-neer*

Gullinbursti: *goo-lin-burst-ee*

Gullveig: *gool-vague*

Heimdall: *hame-dahl*

Hel: *hel*

Hermod: *hehr-mood*

Hod: *hawd*

Hoenir: *hoe-neer*

Idunn: *ee-doon*

Jotunheim: *yoh-tun-hame*

Jotun: *yoh-tun*

Logi: *low-gee*

Loki: *low-key*

Megingjord: *meg-en-yord*

Midgard: *mid-gahrd*

Mimir: *mee-meer*

Mjollnir: *mee-ohl-neer*

Muspell: *moos-pel*

Naglfar: *na-gel-far*

Nanna: *nah-nah*

Nidavellir: *need-ah-vel-ear*

Nidhogg: *need-hog*

Niflheim: *niff-el-hame*

Njord: *nyoord*

Norns: *nornz*

Odin: *oh-din*

Ragnarok: *rahg-nah-rock*

Ratatosk: *rah-tah-tosk*

Sif: *seef*

Sigyn: *seh-gen*

Skadi: *skah-dee*

Skidbladnir: *skee-blahd-neer*

Skirnir: *skeer-neer*

Skrymir: *skree-meer*

Sleipnir: *slep-neer*

Snorri Sturluson: *snor-ee ster-loo-sun*

Sons of Ivaldi: *sons of ee-valh-dee*

Surt: *soort*

Svartalfheim: *svart-alf-hame*

Thialfi: *thee-al-fee*

Thiazi: *thee-ah-see*

Thor: *thor*

Thrym: *thrim*

Tyr: *teer*

Ull: *ool*

Urd: *oord*

Utgard: *oot-gahrd*

Valhalla: *vahl-hahl-ah*

Váli: *vah-lee*

Valkyries: *vahl-kur-reez*

Vanaheim: *vah-nah-hame*

Vanir: *vah-neer*

Ve: *vay*

Vidar: *vee-dahr*

Vili: *vi-lee*

Yggdrasil: *egg-drah-seeil*

Ymir: *ee-meer*